STARTLED

from their graves...

STARTLED

from their graves...

GHOSTS OF MICHIGAN

by Jan Langley

CAPTAIN AND HARRY L.L.C.
Harbor Beach, Michigan

Published by Captain and Harry L.L.C.
Harbor Beach, Michigan

First printing May 2011

19 18 17 16 15   2 3 4 5 6

ISBN 978-0-9724777-2-7

Written by Jan Langley
Interior photos by author except where credited.
Cover Illustration:
Original Oil Painting by Dawn Schumacher
Book layout & design by Julie Taylor

Printed in the United States of America
by McNaughton & Gunn, Inc.

"*The times have been that, when the brains were out, the man would die, and there an end; but now they rise again.*"
—Macbeth

Table of Contents

Introduction

Many people pass on quietly to their eternity, and then there are those who are startled from their graves. Resting in Peace is not their idea of the hereafter. What binds their spirit to this earthly abode can be many things. Perhaps the departed left suddenly and are not quite sure they are, in fact, dead; on the other hand, a house they once lived in and loved might be under restoration and they do not like it. Not one bit. Some spirits are insistent their earthly home remain the same as it was in their lifetime and will do everything they can to make sure that it does. This includes scaring you to death! That lovely broach that they were once so fond of, given to them by a beloved husband or lover, has been auctioned off to a lady to wear on her silly pink sweater. This triggers the return of the spirit from its grave who wants it back. According to Trent Brandon author of *The Ghost Hunters Bible*, "There are individuals with a tremendous love of life. To them, death is a complete shock. These souls seem to refuse to let go of life. They refuse to go off to the other side and instead remain here on earth frequenting fond places from their life."

They seem quite content to repeat their lifetime behaviors such as swinging on a porch swing, watching you from a window or hitchhiking to eternity on a favorite highway. Sometimes a glimpse of a ghost is unexpectedly caught in an ordinary place such as encountering your dead uncle standing directly in front of you as you climb the stairs at your grandmother's house, or as you turn on the lights and enter the dining room in your new home, there sitting at the table is a long dead someone. Then they are gone, leaving a misty cold spot, or the smell of a cigar, or favorite perfume or the lingering stench of a corpse.

That there are ghosts among us is undeniable. I know. I have seen their misty substances and their shadows. I have smelled the odors that they drag from their graves along with them. I have watched their antics, their ringing of bells and moving furniture. I have seen the result of their efforts of trying to manifest. Yes, ghosts are among us, but I will not attempt to make you a believer. Trust me, you have to encounter one, and then you too will be a believer in the afterlife... the netherworld.

The following tales are the result of interviews and investigations. Some are enhanced to scare you to death. Several of them required historical research, especially the Point aux Barques Lighthouse and the Whitefish Point Lighthouse where phantom footsteps follow tourists as they poke their noses into places long-unoccupied by the living. Several phantoms were found in Huron County along M-25. There were great fires in this area, and many people died in the conflagrations of 1871 and 1881. Remember the mysterious orbs that traveled M-28 in my first book, *A Ghostly Road Tour of Michigan's Upper Peninsula?* You will find these same orbs in ditches along the back roads in Michigan's Huron County. Many people believe they are spirits of the people who died in the fires.

In my search for interesting hauntings, several more ghosts were surprised from their graves in the Upper Peninsula: Sault Ste. Marie, Whitefish Point, Delta County's Ford River area, Ispheming, Houghton, and Marquette. You will not find a village or small town in Michigan that does not have its share of ghosts in its houses, saloons, restaurants, museums, theaters, hardware stores, and churches.

Do ghosts have a separate reality other than our imagination? You decide as you read the following accounts of regular people and their encounters with the supernatural. When you least expect it, you too will encounter a ghost. I can almost hear your screams.

Chapter 1

Christmas Spirit

The house was quite large but cozy enough, at least on the main floor which held a large stone fireplace that divided the dining room and living room. The library stood off to the side of the dining room and also had a fireplace and a wonderful view of the back yard; it would be a great place for a cozy fire and a good book. The kitchen was small but filled with storage cupboards and all of the cooking necessities one could want. Mary especially liked the two ovens built into the brick-faced wall beside the stove. The kitchen looked as if it had been redone about ten years before. A central staircase led up to four bedrooms, two on each side of the stairway with a small hallway separating them.

Mike was in the process of finishing off part of the basement to make it into an office. It was one of several remodeling projects they were planning. An old piano remained down there, left behind after the estate sale of the previous owner. Mary often played it while waiting for the dryer to finish its job in the adjacent laundry room.

A few weeks before Christmas, Mary went down to the basement to finish some laundry. After folding the clothes, she set the basket at the bottom of the steps and went to the piano to practice for the holiday recital at her church. Just as she sat down, she heard a soft crying in the wall right next to her. Thoroughly startled, she paused as the notes of "Noel" disappeared into the room. Her fingers turned ice-cold and, improbably, she could see her breath. The weeping started again, very softly... quite close to her as if someone were sitting on the piano bench next to her. That and her frozen fingers jarred her enough to make her run to the stairway grabbing the basket of laundry as she threw herself up the steps. Mike, who was making himself a sandwich in the kitchen, heard the sobbing that seemed to bounce off the walls and echo all around him. He ran to the basement door just in time to catch Mary as she ran into his arms; the laundry basket took flight across the room to land sliding next to the kitchen table where its contents started to unfold and unseen hands pitched them from the basket throughout the room.

This wasn't the first time that strange things had taken place in the house at the end of a country lane outside of a college town in the Upper Peninsula. As a matter of fact, there had been several instances of paranormal activity in the house since Mike and Mary had purchased the property from the Mattsom estate. For the first few months, the activity was limited to slamming doors, flickering lights, and finding an occasional few pots and pans scattered about on the kitchen floor. The activity had only recently increased as Christmas approached. Today's episode was terribly unnerving for Mary. She knew now that their home was haunted. She repeatedly told Mike of the shadowy figure she caught out of the corner of her eye as she sat in the rocking chair in the living room reading her favorite mystery writer, Agatha Christie.

Mike listened but brushed it all off as nerves, but secretly, he too became increasingly aware of unusual occurrences while in the house... especially lately as his tools began to disappear and reappear from one place to another. While they were both a bit unnerved by this latest aberration, they decided to wait until after the Christmas holidays to do anything about it. Their sleep was undisturbed during this time period. Doors stayed shut, lights stayed on, the pots and pans remained in the cupboards. Everything was quiet as if the house were resting.

The week before Christmas they drove to the tree farm about six miles down the road to pick out a Christmas tree. It had started to snow when they pulled their pickup into the parking lot. Holiday music filled the air. Christmas lights were strung throughout the large lot dividing it into sections of small, medium, and large trees. Harry Brown, the owner, greeted them with hand outstretched, "Merry Christmas, you two," he said. "Welcome to the town. Folks around here were glad to hear someone had moved into the old Mattsom place. Everything going fine there?"

"It's a great house," answered Mike.

"We love it," Mary added.

"Yep," replied Harry, "Cara Lee was the last of the Mattsoms. They owned the property for generations. Fine family. Bit strange in their thinking on some things, but a real fine family. So how big a tree you folks want? I got 'em all sizes."

"Not too tall," said Mary looking around as she walked over to some nicely shaped evergreens. "Like this one. This is the right size," she added as she brushed snow from its branches. "What do you think, Mike?"

Harry walked over and grabbed the tree, picked it up and put it down hard. "Here," he said, "Walk 'round it. Got a nice shape, doesn't it?"

"Perfect," announced Mary. While Harry tied the tree to the back end of the pickup, Mary prodded, "What did you mean when you said the Mattsoms had some strange ideas?"

"Didn't mean nothing, just sometimes they were different from us in their thinking," replied Harry. "Use to tell stories about the house and the stuff going on there… you know. Ghosts. Nothing to it, of course, but they never moved out so guess it was all their imaginations now, wasn't it?" Harry answered as he turned to another family that had just pulled in.

"Well, now you folks have a nice Christmas and enjoy that tree. Be sure to water it good every day now, you hear?" he said as he tipped his hat to them and walked over to a family with two small kids. "Hi there," he called as he walked into the group and Mike pulled out of the lot.

"Now what do you suppose that was all about?" asked Mary as they drove the short distance home.

"Beats me. Seems like the Mattsoms, according to Harry, were a little off the norm, but then again, maybe they were right. I mean... well, lets face it, Mary, there is something about that house we're in."

Mary shivered, "I know... but darn it, Mike, I really like the old place. And it's perfect for us. It really is. By time we're done with it, it will be a showplace," said Mary as they pulled up to the garage.

Mike took the Christmas tree into the garage to cut off the bottom while Mary went to locate the ornaments. After moving into the old house, she recalled she had seen old boxes of ornaments in the basement storage room or the attic, and she remembered being excited about maybe finding some real antique Christmas decorations. She first went down into the basement, forgetting her fear of her last trip. As she switched on the lights, she thought she saw a movement near the piano. Suddenly, she was chilled to the bone and she turned and ran back up the stairs, through the kitchen, and into the garage and safety where Mike was just putting the tree into the stand. "What's up, Mary? Anything wrong?"

"Mike, I'll wait for you to come down to the basement with me and look for our decorations. You did put them down there, didn't you?"

"Nope, they're here in the garage. Up there," he pointed. "See those three large boxes next to the window? I'll get them for you in a minute; now show me where you want this beast in the house."

She laughed, "My goodness, I think it grew while it was in the back of the truck. Let's try the living room first; just follow me." The tree went directly in front of the large bay window in the living room. It seemed to be the perfect spot. Mike carried in the boxes of decorations while Mary brought in hot chocolate and sandwiches. "I remember seeing some old boxes of Christmas ornaments in the basement, Mike, but honestly, after my last trip down there, I would rather you come with me. Do you mind?" she giggled as she glanced over at him, then said, "Maybe you should start doing the wash for me too." He gave her "the look."

A short time later, when their snack had disappeared, they cautiously followed the steps into the basement. Mary found the boxes she remembered behind the furnace on some shelves covered with dust. They pulled them out and carried them upstairs without incident.

By the time darkness arrived, the tree was lighted and covered with the old ornaments from their previous home. The older ornaments that had come from the basement seemed to glow with an inner light, but Mary knew that was just her imagination and laughed at her ability to turn something beautiful into something spooky. Mike gathered Mary into his arms as they stood looking at the tree. Dinner took just a little time to prepare; meanwhile, snow had started falling and it was covering the surrounding landscape with a thick blanket, not at all unusual for this part of the Upper Peninsula. The fireplace threw shadows dancing on the walls and ceiling as they returned to the living room to catch the news and

Mike and Mary's Christmas tree in the living room.

weather on TV 6. It was Mary who first noticed something was missing from the tree.

"Mike," she asked, "why does the tree look different?"

"Different? How?" he answered.

"I don't know, it just looks different." They both stared at the tree. The wind started to blow, and they could hear it crying through the tall pines that lined the drive. Suddenly, Mary shivered as she moved closer to Mike. "Mike," she whispered, "they are all gone..." Her voice drifted off into silence. And they were all gone. All of the old ornaments found behind the furnace were gone. But where did they go and how did they go?

They both heard or thought they heard a soft giggle, a whisper of laughter that seemed to dance around the tree.

"Mike, I am scared," whimpered Mary, clinging to his arm as they climbed the stairs to bed. Mary locked the bedroom door. Silly, she thought, as if that would keep out a ghost.

The following morning, after coffee and a discussion on what to do next, they decided to begin searching the house for the missing ornaments. They made their way downstairs to the basement and started behind the furnace. As Mary looked through the old cupboards, she felt an icy cold wrap around her like a shroud; the lights flickered off–on–off again. "Mike," she said in a voice above a whisper. "Mike!" she cried out a bit louder. She slowly forced herself to turn around and face the stairway. "Mike," she insisted in a pitiful call for help.

"I can see her," Mike answered in a stunned voice. A white-haired lady wearing a silvery dress stood at the bottom of the steps. In her hand she held one of the missing ornaments. She smiled and turned to walk upstairs, vanishing as she went.

"Oh my God, Mike, who was that?"

"I believe that was the former Cara Lee Mattsom," answered Mike. "Come upstairs, I found something in the garage the other day that I forgot to tell you about."

Mary trailed Mike up the stairs into the kitchen. "Sit here, honey, while I go get it." Once again Mary grew cold. Icy fingers of frost spread across her back, up her arms and neck. She quickly got up and watched in amazement as the same lady appeared in front of her… but this time she was pointing to the library. She seems so sad thought Mary as she slowly walked into the library. There on a chair, neatly stacked, sat the boxes with the old Christmas ornaments. She took one out of its wrapping when Mike reappeared exclaiming, "You found them!"

"Not me, Mike. The spirit pointed me to them. What have you got?"

Mike kept looking at the boxes of ornaments in wonder as he replied, "It's an old album."

They sat on the floor next to the fireplace and opened the large leather-bound book with *Christmas* engraved on the front. It was filled with photos of children playing in the snow, horses pulling sleds, and Christmas trees. Scrolled beneath each Christmas tree was the date. The earliest was 1871. The tin types and photos were not taken in the living room but rather... was it the library?

"How strange, Mike. Notice where they have placed the tree through the years?" She answered for him, "Every one pictured has the tree here in the library."

A small push of air seemed to slip across the room making the flames in the fireplace dance a two-step. "You know, Mary, you're right. I wonder though, why here?" He got up and walked around the room looking at the book-lined walls. The large stained-glass window in the room held a window seat and overlooked the back yard.

"It looks like the trees were always placed in front of this window," said Mary.

"Yeah, and away from the fireplace," he answered as he continued his probing. Mary placed another log on the fire.

She walked over to the window shivering as she looked out at the frozen landscape. Mike's voice startled her as he cried out, "Mary! Look at this!"

"God, Mike, scare me to death why don't you... what have you found?"

"The answer to the mystery of this room and the Christmas tree," he slowly replied as he pushed books aside on both ends of the bookcases opposite the fireplace.

"A secret room?" asked Mary.

"No, no secret room. Look here, Mary. This room used to be the main living area. You can tell by the original molding behind the books. This is the original house. Our living room is... for Pete's sake, an addition!"

"So, Mike, our Christmas tree belongs in here. It's a family tradition." As she spoke the pages of the Christmas album that lay open in front of them slowly began to turn. Mike sat next to Mary as they watched in amazement.

"What the...!" exclaimed Mike.

"Shusssssssh," cautioned Mary.

Suddenly, the boxes of ornaments that sat forgotten on the chair fell to the floor and scattered through the room. At the same time, the pages stopped. The book lay open to a picture of a white-haired lady watching a small girl placing an ornament on the tree. Beneath the picture was written, *Cara Lee and Great Grandmother Caroline Mattsom, 1939.* As they looked closely, they could see the ornaments on the tree in the picture were the very ornaments that lay spread beneath their feet.

"Well, I guess we know what we have to do to make things right around here," said Mary as she got up and went into the living room with Mike close behind.

"We'll have to keep up the tradition," replied Mike with a smile on his face.

It took the rest of the evening before they finally sat down in the library with a glass of wine, admiring the newly placed Christmas tree in front of the library window.

"I guess that wasn't Cara Lee we saw," said Mike.

"No, not Cara Lee but Caroline. She was concerned the traditions would be forgotten."

Caroline Mattsom never again reappeared in the old house. But often, as Christmas nears, an ornament mysteriously appears in the oddest of places: in a silverware drawer, on the porch swing, in a shoe, and once in the dog's bed. But never in the living room. The appearance of the ornaments signals it is time to purchase a Christmas tree for the holidays.

Chapter 2

The Deer Camp Spirit

The Deer Stalkers

A group of men would meet once a year at a hunting camp located near the Peshikee Grade near Ishpeming. Three of them were retired Ford Motor Company employees, who had held positions of responsibility in the company. They loved to hunt in the Upper Peninsula.

The camp looked like most hunting camps throughout Michigan with a fridge to keep the beer cold, a stove to make the camp stew, several cots, a wood stove to keep warm, and a table for the poker games.

They usually gathered at John's place prior to leaving for camp. John, along with his wife Sandy, had returned to the UP after he had retired. John and Sandy only lived an hour's drive from the camp.

At this time of year, the local grocery stores are always well stocked for the onslaught of hunters that spend big bucks trying to get that "big buck." It was a good area to shop and gather supplies such as backpacks, sleeping bags, ammunition, hatchets, and toilet paper for the outhouse along with food supplies.

A few days before the big day, John, along with a pair of brothers, Frank, who came down to join them from Sault Ste. Marie, and Rob, from Calumet, left town and headed for the camp with a full truckload of provisions. Gordy and Rick, coming up from downstate, would arrive the following afternoon. Their arrival would complete the group that called themselves "The Deer Stalkers."

Spirits were high; fellowship was in the air as they unloaded their supplies. The wind had turned to the north the day before; it brought a Hudson Bay chill to the air that rushed over the peninsula. "Maybe snow by tomorrow," called John to Rob as they emptied the pickup.

"That would be great..." Rob answered, "...for tracking."

"Hey, you guys," Frank hollered from the camp doorway, "where did you put the chili pot?"

"On the table..." called John.

"Can't make chili without a pot," grumbled Frank.

"It's on the damn table. Put the beer down and open your eyes!" shouted John.

Frank walked down the steps and over to John, who was about to carry a huge box to the porch.

"OK, John. Good joke. There is no chili pot on the table, no chili pot on the stove, no chili pot on the sink, on the couch, on the anything. There is no chili pot anywhere. So where in hell did you put the chili pot?"

John walked up to the porch while Frank was hollering in his ear. He put down the box, straightened up, walked into the camp and over to the table, and picked up the chili pot. "Right here!" said John.

Frank was silent. He looked at the chili pot, at John, and back at the chili pot. "That's impossible," he murmured as he shook his head in disbelief.

A while later, after finishing emptying the pickup, Rob called out to Frank, "How's that chili coming?"

"I need the onions. You guys unload the onions yet?" answered Frank.

"Got it in here," replied Rob as he started to unpack the last large box. "Here it is, and everything else you will need except the hot peppers. I gotta find the potatoes and peppers," he said as he started to unpack the rest of the boxes.

They finished their dinner of chili and burgers around 9:00 that night. John started the wood stove and then piled wood on the porch next to the door. Frank went out to the porch, sat on one of the old rocking chairs, and lit a cigar where Rob joined him. "Funny about that chili pot," said Frank.

"Aw, you just missed it in the rush to unpack," answered Rob.

John joined them with a cigarette in one hand and a cold beer in the other. "Forget the pot. I think we've got everything we need. You guys think of anything we're missing?"

"Yeah, a couple hands of poker and another beer," answered Rob.

They awoke the following morning to a light snowfall. It was a perfect start to the week thought Frank, the designated cook, as he made pancakes and fried up some sausage while Rob and John walked out about a half a mile into the woods to check out the deer blinds. In the meantime, Frank heard someone come up the porch steps and the sound of stomping feet. Good, he thought, Gordy and Rick are here. He turned to the door waiting to greet them.

"Come on in, guys," he called. No one answered. He put the last of the pancakes into the oven to be kept warm and walked out to the porch. No one was there. There were no footprints on the snow-covered steps. Nothing. The woods were quiet as a cemetery. A chill ran up his spine as he slowly turned his head at a movement near the edge of the woods. Was that a hunter walking away, he asked himself?

"Hey you!" he called. There was no reply. The figure was gone. He raced down the steps to the place where he thought he saw—what had he seen?

He searched for footsteps in the snow but found nothing. I need a beer, he thought and did not care if it was not noon. It was noon somewhere he figured.

A few minutes later with a beer in his hand, Frank heard the voices of John and Rob coming up the two-track.

"About time you two got back here. The pancakes will taste like hardtack if you don't eat them now." He did not mention the footsteps or the disappearing hunter. Along with Gordy and Rick, the afternoon brought more snow. Their arrival signaled it was time for Frank to start the camp stew. After unloading more gear, the group, with testosterone running high, gathered around the table for sandwiches and cold beer as they planned their strategy for the following morning's Opening Day. Frank, while keeping up with the conversation, continued to add onions, garlic, carrots, and the kitchen stove to the pot of camp stew. As the afternoon waned, the men decided to split up and walk the woods in search of buck signs. Gordy and John walked toward the bluff that ran along the north edge of the forty. The dim sunlight pushed through the darkened branches of the trees and made a multi-colored carpet of fallen leaves that left little evidence of their passing. Rob and Rick confined their search to the low ground, a melting of swamp and tag alders. Frank, once again back at camp, was in the outhouse conducting his daily business when he heard a gruff voice call, "Hurry up in there!"

Frank laughed and replied. "Gotta do what I gotta do!" There was no reply. Frank slowly opened the outhouse door. A low mist was spreading its fingers across the forest floor as he slowly walked over to the camp porch. "Damn," he said aloud. "Who was that?" As he approached the porch, he saw another hunter sitting in the rocking chair smoking a pipe. "Oh, it was you..." he called out as he got closer. The hunter turned toward him, smiled, and slowly melted into the surrounding mist.

He walked up the steps. What the hell was that about, he asked himself. His heart pounded against his rib cage as he went through the doorway to stir the pot of stew. His hands were sweating as he opened a beer, went back on the porch, lit a cigar, and waited for the crew to return. Taking his last sip, he heard the men coming through the tall brush.

They were excited; they found deer markings all over. Their faces were flushed as they took turns slapping each other on the back. Frank sat quietly at the table until they finally noticed his demeanor.

"What's with you, Frank?" asked John.

Frank answered, "Did you guys see any other hunters when you were out there?"

"Didn't see a soul," John answered.

"Me either," said Rob.

As clouds darkened the sky and twilight slipped into darkness, Rob and Gordy cleared the table from their stew dinner while Frank loaded the stove with firewood. Looking over at his brother, Rob, he asked if anyone had ever died at the camp.

"Not that I know of," Rob answered. "Why?"

Frank didn't reply.

"Ask John," said Rob, "he should know."

The camp door slammed behind John as he carried in a load of firewood.

"Hey John," Rob questioned, "anyone ever die out here at the camp?"

John, taking his time piling the wood in the wood box, replied slowly, "Why?"

The question went unanswered as the group pulled up chairs around the table for a short night of poker; nobody slept in on Opening Day. While playing another winning hand, Rick told them a story of Opening Day when he lived up in Munising. "One of the old timers went to Seney to the Mennonite store over there to pick up three or four 25-pound bags of dog food couple weeks before the season opened.

PHOTO COURTESY OF BRAD BLAIR

Every few days he spread that dog food all around his blind. Opening day that year was warm, and a thick fog blanketed the woods, but the old timer got his buck anyways. Apparently he just aimed at the barking." Laughter filled the room as they asked Frank if he had any dog food in the cupboards.

A sudden frigid chill filled the cabin wrapping its finger of frost around the men's legs and backs. The light over the table dimmed and went out. Cards flew off the table as dishes spilled from the cupboard. Rob grabbed for the flashlight on the table behind him as John felt his chair being pulled backwards; he landed sideways, still holding his beer upright—a sign of a true Yooper. The lights came back on. The cold was gone. They all stood where they were as if frozen in time. Gordy broke the silence.

"What the hell was that?" he asked.

"There's no earthquakes in the UP," grumbled Rick.

John lit a cigarette as he walked to the door. "Just another UFO taking off," laughed Rob.

"I thought they were all over near Craig Lake," replied Frank.

"Another UFO… too many beers," added John. "Let's get some sleep."

Before daylight, the group made its way into the woods to their various deer stands. A hushed stillness crept over the land, waiting for sunrise. Frank wondered at the deep shadow that moved slightly ahead of him as he made his way to his blind. Was it a deer? Or one of the guys? Meanwhile, John and Rob made their silent way to the ridge as Gordy and Rick waited for daybreak near the edge of the swamp. Gordy watched an unknown hunter melt into the tag alders ahead of him.

As Frank waited for the dim sunlight of a frosty dawn, he was deep in thought. As a member of the UPPRS (The Upper Peninsula Paranormal Research Society) in his hometown of Sault Ste. Marie, camp this year had all the earmarks of a haunting. A sudden snap of a branch alerted him to a presence behind him. He slowly turned to find a fog-like outline of an elderly hunter walking toward him. Frank whispered, "Who are you?" The figure seemed to wave at him as it turned and disappeared into the tree line. Suddenly, a buck darted from the tree line as if spooked and ran directly towards him. Frank watched in amazement as it stopped its wild dash a mere ten feet directly in front of him. It turned and continued its mad dash down the slope and back into the woods. He put his gun down. He sat on an old upright log and pulled out a cigarette. The sun was up. Shots echoed from the direction of the swamp.

He sat quietly for another hour before giving up for the afternoon and headed back toward the camp. Walking down hill, he ran into John; they followed the two-track though the woods.

"Any luck, John?" he asked.

"Nothing," John answered. "Heard shots from over near the swamp, but I never saw a thing."

They continued on their way.

"Who is he, John?" Frank asked.

John stopped. "What do you mean?" John replied.

"Who is the ghost that's haunting the camp, that's what I mean."

"What the hell are you saying, Frank?"

"Come on, John, I've seen him. Not once but a couple of times and…" he continued, "back there he just walked out of the woods towards me. Scared up a buck when he did. That's what I mean," said Frank grabbing John's arm.

John stopped. He cupped his hand around a cigarette, inhaled, and released the smoke through his nose answering, "I think it's my great-grandfather. He built the place back in the early 1900s. He was always camp cook, which probably explains why you are seeing him. All the years I've been up here with my dad and then my boys, I never saw nothing, but this summer I took a ride up here just to check things out. Just as I pulled up, I saw something sitting in the old rocking chair on the porch—scared the hell out of me. Recognized him when I saw him again about a week later when I came up to chop some wood."

"Why would he be here?" asked Frank.

"I've been thinking about it, and the only thing I can figure is Sandy and I been talking about selling the place. We only use it anymore when all of us get together. It's worth a pretty bundle in today's market. I figured I was the only one that could see him, but I should have known you would figure something was wrong up here, you being with that bunch of ghost hunters from the Sault and all."

"I wonder if any of the other guys have seen him?" said Frank.

"No one has said anything to me. Hey look! Gordy and Rick are back. It figures—they're sitting on the porch with a beer. You guys leave any for us?" called John as they approached.

They made sandwiches for lunch while Frank put a huge roast in the oven. Rick helped him peel potatoes and threw them in the pot to join the onions and carrots. "There, that'll be ready for us tonight when we get back here," he said.

"With all the tracks out there, where in hell are all the deer?" asked Rob.

"I heard shooting but never saw a deer, not even the tail-end of one. Saw another hunter out there though. He disappeared into the woods. Must be a neighbor. Anyone else see him?" Gordy questioned. John and Frank looked at each other.

They left the camp again around mid-afternoon and once again returned empty-handed at dark. Frank was the first to arrive back, and he noticed all the lights were on as he walked up the two-track. Someone beat me back, he thought to himself. When he opened the door, however, the camp was vacant. Whoever had been there earlier had set the table for their dinner. Frank heard a chuckle behind him. He turned to find the old man sitting in the chair next to the potbelly stove. A full-bodied apparition, thought Frank. The Holy Grail of ghost hunting and I don't have a freaking camera. The vision faded as Frank heard the calls of the other guys as they came back to the camp. Frank met them at the front door.

"What's the matter with you, Frank, you look like you've seen a ghost," laughed Rob as he entered.

All of them made their way inside, removing jackets, taking off boots, going out on the porch for a smoke, and out to the outhouse; they were a jumble of orange. John moved next to Frank and asked what had happened. Frank told him about the apparition in the chair, the lights, and the table being set. John shook his head while saying, "That's enough. I need to talk to Sandy. We can't sell this place, not if the old boy is going to keep dragging his butt back here to scare the hell out of all of us."

The week ended with the group in high spirits. They got their bucks, that is, all of them except Frank. He didn't care. He caught something more important—a full-bodied ghost— and he couldn't wait to tell the guys up in the Sault about his experience!

The Deer Stalkers continue to return every year to hunt the "big one," tell jokes, drink beer, and play poker. John and Frank have never seen the apparition again. Apparently, John and Sandy's decision to keep the camp has reassured the old boy and he has taken his ass back to eternity where he belongs.

Chapter 3

The Ford River Haunting

*N*ear the Ford River in Delta County, Dan and Shirley were renting a small house at the end of a county road. They had three boys; the two older ones were eleven and thirteen and the youngest was four. The older boys had three wheelers and were allowed to go through the woods to the next mile and back.

One late, warm fall afternoon, Dan stopped to talk to Frank, the owner of the property, who lived about a quarter of a mile down the road in a two-story brick home. He had bought the property and built the house for his dear wife in the early '40s. Frank told Dan how much he enjoyed the boys when they stopped by for a visit and, usually, a snack. Dan was upset that the boys were bothering the old man, but Frank insisted that their visits were no problem, and, as a matter of fact, he quite looked forward to them especially since he had lost his wife during this past year. He walked over to the porch steps and sat down. Dan joined him. "I'm going to move, Dan, to Arizona, to live with my daughter. Going to put the place here up for sale." Dan's heart sank knowing he would surely have to leave the rental. He asked Frank the price of the property. He knew he could never afford it.

About a month later, just before Christmas, Frank again approached Dan telling him how much he would like to see Dan and his family have the property. He told Dan it was the perfect place to raise a family. "I'll lower my price for you,

Dan, if you agree to buy it in the spring." After several long conversations with each other and the bank, they agreed to purchase the big house, the rental, and the ten acres. Frank left for Arizona after the paperwork was completed. He would never return.

The family moved to the big house on the first of April. It was the perfect home for them—a couple of acres, large garage and storage sheds, and the boys each had their own bedrooms—even the youngest, who was now five, had his own room across the hall from his parents. Frank had told them it was the room where his wife Helen had kept all of her hobby projects and her collection of books and dolls. At that time, he had assured them he would have all of her things removed when they bought the house. Nevertheless, when moving day arrived, the room was just as it had been before Frank left. He just never got around to cleaning it out.

It was mid-July when the youngest boy started to complain that a lady, "I think her name is Helen, Mom." kept waking him up. She wanted to hold him and tell him stories, but he wanted to sleep. Dan and Shirley did not think much of his complaints at the time. After all, he was adjusting to his new room and that takes time. His complaints grew louder as the summer wore on. One day he told his mom, as he sat at the kitchen table eating a peanut butter sandwich and downing it with a tall glass of milk, the lady liked to pat his head and, he continued, "She takes up all of the room on my bed when she sits down, and she throws my books on the floor when I don't want to listen to another story," he grumbled. Shirley paused for a minute, turned and looked at the boy, and thought, he just wants attention. He certainly did not like sleeping in a room all alone. Leaving the safety of the small bed next to Dan and Shirley was proving to be a big adjustment for the little boy. He told his brothers about the lady and they just laughed.

"We'll come and sleep with you, scaredy-cat. We'll scare her away!" they teased. And they did, but nothing happened, just the window opened up by itself to let a cold breeze whisper through the room. The boys giggled and pulled the covers up over their heads.

Helen kept visiting the little boy all that fall. He adjusted to her attentions, if it is possible to adjust yourself to visitations by a ghost. He no longer mentioned her antics as frequently to his family.

Meanwhile, Frank had passed away in Arizona. A memorial was held for him at the local funeral home. Flowers and memorabilia from his life surrounded an urn that held his ashes. Dan, Shirley, and the boys attended the memorial service. As they reached the memorial table, the youngest boy stopped and pointed to a picture next the urn. "Look, Mom, that's the lady that visits me at night. That's Helen!" It was a picture of Helen and Frank, taken at their 50th Wedding Anniversary party. Apparently, Helen had waited for Frank to join her in eternity for she never visited the youngest boy again. The older boys often mention seeing a guy that reminds them of Frank walking with a woman in a blue dress through the woods, but they are always so far away that the boys have never managed to find them.

Chapter 4

Recollections of a Haunting

*A*s a young child, Alice remembers living in Detour. At least once a year, her parents would hook up the horses to the wagon for a trip up to the Sault to visit with her great-grandmother and great-grandfather.

It was around 1855, when commerce had grown quickly after the system of the two original locks had been completed. By the 1870s, however, the need for additional new locks became clear. She remembers it was about a two-day trip. When the uncles and aunts heard they were coming, they decided they would also arrive at the great-grandparent's house for a get-together before the snows came to that part of the peninsula. The great-grandparents had a house on Portage Street. At that time, there were many houses along the street and a few boarding houses too.

When they arrived, the women would gather in the kitchen around the large table with their knitting and tea while the men were sent to the shed to smoke their pipes and talk about the building of the locks and all of the strangers in town. Alice remembers as if it were yesterday, she was sitting next to her mother on a small stool holding a doll one of the aunts had given her. The house was quiet, and only the murmur of the soft talk of the aunts could be heard in the kitchen. It was dark outside, and the flicker of the oil lamp was putting her to sleep. The sound of heavy footsteps could be heard coming up stairs from the cellar. Everyone got quiet. The group of women listened as they held their breaths. Suddenly, Great-grandmother stood up and shouted into the silence, "Now listen, you, don't you come up here tonight! Do you hear me? You go right back downstairs where you belong!"

Alice sat up and leaned into her mother's lap. A hushed silence filled the room. Then... hesitatingly... the footsteps started again. It seemed as if they were right on the other side of the cellar door.

"Stop right there!" Great-grandmother shouted. The footsteps stopped.

Great-grandmother ran to the back porch calling to her husband, "He's back! Get in here and tell him to leave! I've got company, damn his dirty soul." Great-grandfather came rushing through the back door and pushed on the cellar door, and the door bulged as it pushed back. By now, everyone in the kitchen had scrambled out of their seats and stood back against the hallway door.

Alice huddled between her aunts and clung to her mother's dress. Her doll lay forgotten on the floor under the table. Her great-grandfather spoke quietly to whatever was on the other side of that door.

"Just go back," he said in a voice just above a whisper, "and we'll talk about this later."

"I thought that ghost had left here," said one of the uncles that formed a group by the back door.

"Well, he doesn't bother no one, and we feel kinda bad for him being trapped here on this side of perdition so we let him stay," answered Great-grandfather.

"He ain't gonna stay if he can't leave my company alone!" cried Great-grandmother.

"He's just curious more than likely," said Great-grandfather, "just curious and probably a little lonely. We figure he used to be a logger who used to live here when it was a boarding house. We've been told a logger got himself killed right here in this kitchen. They threw his body down in the cellar and then buried him there. We don't know if it's the truth or just a tale. We did find some bones down there. We gave them a decent burial in the yard by the fence. Even said a prayer over 'em."

Alice's mother grabbed her arm and dragged her to the upstairs bedroom where they were going to sleep. She stood by helplessly as she watched her mother throw their belongings into a satchel and followed her back down the darkened stairway. They slept in the parlor that night along with several of the aunts and left for home early the next morning. The doll remained forgotten under the kitchen table. Silence was heavy between her parents as they traveled back home. Alice remembers it was snowing.

It was another two years, in the spring, that her great-grandparents sold that house and moved farther down the river. Much later, when her great-grandfather was dying, her parents drove the wagon to their farmhouse. Her mother and father were sitting with her great-grandmother on the porch when Alice decided to go and see her great-grandfather. He was in a bedroom down a long, dark hallway. She slipped silently into the room to sit next to him by his bed. He was a little old man by then, and she patted his hand softly to let him know she was there. He died right in front of her, and she watched smoke-like stuff come out of his mouth and disappear into the room; she knew it was his spirit. She started to cry. She often thinks about that logger and wonders if he ever did get to the other side or if he is still haunting that old cellar.

Chapter 5

The House Had Always Been Haunted

The house looked quite small from the lane, but it rambled on in bits and pieces for nearly a half of a village block. It had two stories with staircases at the north and south ends. Five bedrooms were strung out through small doorways that wound through the upstairs. The downstairs had a huge front room said, at one time, to have been a funeral parlor; it connected to another bedroom, probably an office for the business of the dead. Both were separated from the rest of the living quarters by double doors that opened into a dining room, parlor, and the entry to the south stairway. Beyond the parlor, the large kitchen melted into the pantry, and tucked behind the pantry was the north staircase. The house had always been haunted.

There were stories, told by the great-great-grandmother, that went back to before World War I of the spirits that wandered the hallways of the old house. Crouched in an overstuffed chair in the parlor next to the oil burner, the old lady would pick up her knitting and retell the stories of long-past paranormal experiences of herself, her mother and her grandmother, and other members of the family. She would always begin, "I remember… When I was young, my husband was somewhere in Germany during the First World War. One night when the wind was blowing a gale over the lake, I heard a sudden noise by the north stairwell. I woke quickly and crossed to the nursery. I saw a woman there, fully dressed in mourning black, leaning over my baby's crib. I rushed to push her away thinking she had come to steal my baby, but my hands went right through her. The woman then turned from me back to the child. I fell to my knees and started to pray to the Virgin Mary. The woman turned to me again and started to cry. She then melted into the darkness. I brought my baby back to bed with me, and I lay there shivering with cold until dawn. Not long after, a message arrived telling of my husband's death on foreign soil. I had been forewarned," she whispered.

The upstairs of that house is dense with ghosts. Molly, a granddaughter, was sleeping in the upstairs bedroom near the top of the south staircase. She awoke one night, shivering with icy cold drafts that swept across the room. She rolled over and turned to pull up the heavy quilt that had fallen on the floor. As she adjusted the covers, she looked up to see a man standing at the foot of the bed. He was fully dressed in a naval uniform. She knew it was her uncle Frank who drowned three months earlier in a plane crash off the south of France. He smiled at her, then turned and walked to the staircase. Calling out to him, she started to follow, but as she went after him, she found herself walking in water that had spread into a large puddle at the foot of the bed. She screamed with the sudden realization of what she had seen. The hallway lights came on as her mother dashed to her side. Pointing to the water, they both observed the sodden footprints that led down the steps and gradually faded. He was not seen in the house again for a long time. The stories continued through the years with various family members repeating some of the old, but often recounting new experiences. One night, as Virginia, the oldest daughter of Molly, was reading in the downstairs bedroom, she heard weeping coming from outside of her door. She, well aware of the stories of late night phantoms that inhabited the old house, thought to herself as she opened the door, maybe I will finally see a ghost. She pulled the door open to see a roomful of mourners dressed in various shades of black standing around a casket displayed in the center of the room. She stood in shock as she watched them move about, seemingly talking with each other, but not a sound could be heard. She slowly closed the door and leaned against it, her heart pounding in her chest. She gasped for breath and said a quick Hail Mary, then, once again, slowly opened the door. The room was empty. As she quickly and quietly gathered her things into the small bag she had brought with her for her weekend visit, she hesitated and once again opened the door to the old funeral parlor, worried of the specters she might encounter. The room was again empty, but shadows filled the corners and seemed to dart across the room. She never returned to the house.

As old houses go, there are always repairs to be made, adjustments to modern living, things to be torn out, and things to be refurbished. As the family changed from parents to grandparents, the house also changed. Change is something that spirits are not fond of; in fact, they downright disapprove.

When Val and her husband, Cory, the last of the descendants of the original owners, moved in, tales of the haunting had faded into the past. Little did they know that the changes they had made to modernize the house would wake the dead. What they didn't know was the spirited renovations had caused an interruption of the spirit world in the house. It all began as Cory was shaving in the upstairs bathroom. Val, his wife, had insisted on keeping an original round mirror over the sink. As Cory lathered his face, the bathroom door slammed shut. The vibration shook the old mirror. After Cory glanced at the door, his gaze returned to the mirror, but it was not his face that he saw. The mirror swirled with fog forming the face of an ancient woman crying. Startled, he jumped back. His hand grabbed at the towel about his neck. He rubbed the mirror to clear it, but the image remained. What the hell is that? he thought. Slowly the image faded and the mirror returned to normal. He decided not to tell Val. Why scare her? His thoughts raced as he finished his grooming.

He began to dread his morning ritual, for the old lady appeared at regular intervals and eventually he moved his things to the downstairs bathroom. The mirror there behaved like a normal mirror. Later that week, as Val vacuumed the new den (the old parlor), she noticed an odd smell. She changed the vacuum bag, but the smell remained. It was bad. It made her gag. Then, it was gone. She finished the room and turned to move her cleaning supplies into Cory's new office (the old office of the funeral parlor) when, out of the corner of her eye, she thought she saw someone standing by the desk. She turned to the desk to find that a misty haze hovered by the wastebasket. Dust? She was suddenly freezing cold, so much that she could see her breath. The haze moved to the closet and disappeared. She cautiously opened the door, and a musty swirl of dust enveloped her. To her surprise, the closet spilled over with musty black garments. I know we cleaned this out she said to herself. She left the room to find Cory. Not finding him immediately, she retreated to the kitchen for a glass of cool lemonade to clear her head and then made her way to the new deck off the kitchen. Cory was just coming up the steps.

"Notice anything about this house?" she asked.

He laughed and answered, "Nothing surprises me in this old place."

"Well, we do know a few of the old stories about the place, and… I'm wondering, is there some truth to them?" They left the conversation there. She forgot to tell him of the closet full of black garments.

The following day, Cory sat in his office wondering what the horrible smell was that invaded his privacy. He finally got up and walked about the room, following his nose. He opened the door to the new den and felt himself cry out in startled disbelief as he watched a casket carried into the center of the room. A small gathering of mourners surrounded it. The scene faded into smatterings of dust swirls that slowly drifted away into nothing. Meanwhile, Val busied herself cleaning the bedroom at the top of the south stairs only to discover water at the end of the bed. She mopped it up thinking she had tipped the bucket after filling it in the upstairs bathroom. After dusting and remaking the bed there, she was returning to the stairway when she noticed small puddles of water on the steps. Then, she remembered. She remembered the story her grandmother had told them when they were little about the man in the uniform who had appeared at the foot of her aunt's bed. Damn, she thought as she ran down the stairs calling for Cory. They met in the dining room, faces flushed, hearts beating, reaching for each other.

Today, "For Sale" signs decorate the front and side yards. The house has always been haunted.

Chapter 6

Spirits of the Whitefish Point Lighthouse

The Ojibwa woman followed the sunrise's path through the dark pine forest to the shoreline of the bay. She knelt in the sand; tears washed her cheeks as she held her arms out in supplication to the Great Spirit to save her beloved husband from the shadow of death.

Everyday she follows this same ritual; even after his soul had left its earthly bounds, she returns to the shore following the same path... for over two hundred years. Even today she is sometimes seen, when conditions are just right, through the mists that gather on the lighthouse grounds. Sounds have been captured on tape by local ghost hunters of a noise as if someone is walking through tall grass... is it the Indian woman walking to the shore? Many generations ago the Ojibwa spent their summers here at this Gathering Place. That the Indian woman's spirit still lingers is no surprise according to the reports received by the Upper Peninsula Paranormal Research Society (i.e., the UPPRS), who have conducted several investigations of the spirits here at Whitefish. The gift shop, Captain's Quarters, theater, and museum have revealed unexplainable phenomenon. One of the most intriguing is the spirit of a little girl of about six or seven years old. She most often manifests in the upper window of the living quarters of the US Coast Guard's Life Saving Station. One of the early directors of the station had a daughter of that age who died in the living quarters. Is it her spirit peering down from the

Whitefish Point Lighthouse

second floor window? It is believed to be her spirit that is seen walking the grounds wearing period dress and a bonnet, so much so as to provoke a group of tourists to ask an employee at the lighthouse if there was a historical reenactment that day. Of course, there was not.

Near the child's mannequin in the living quarters, the team recorded a four-degree drop in temperature and a darting shadow in the same area. One late afternoon, just as shadows began to deepen, the manager of the lighthouse went into the crew's quarters building to check on it. Feeling somewhat light-headed, she went into the bunkroom and sat on a lower bed. She saw an impression on the covers as though someone was sitting there next to her, then she felt a hand placed gently on her shoulder. She believed it to be the little girl who has been seen so many times throughout the property as if she is searching for her mother or a playmate.

There have been reports of fifty ghosts haunting Whitefish Point Lighthouse. Employees report finding books scattered about the floor of the main office and gift shop. Doors open and close of their own volition and unseen hands flush the toilets.

A maintenance man one day reported he went into the theater early in the morning before it opened and heard a loud conversation in the back. Although he searched the premises, he could not find one living soul; the key word here is "living." He left immediately!

Visitors have reported seeing a woman walking the stairs and the outside walk of the light tower. And, there is a story of a lighthouse keeper who experienced a crisis apparition. His father appeared to him at the foot of his bed at the precise time of his death many miles away.

Tragedy haunts Whitefish Bay. From the sailing schooners of the early 1800s to the loss of the *Edmund Fitzgerald,* a 729-foot ore-freighter in 1975, there is a macabre parade of lost men who have braved the deep, ice-cold waters of Lake Superior and her treacherous rants and rages.

That the unimaginably harsh weather of Lake Superior country, the loneliness, and the fear would leave energies trapped in this desolate yet beautiful place cannot be conceived. The UPPRS will continue their search for the paranormal at Whitefish. May the spirits of all that are here find rest and peace.

Chapter 7

A Residual Haunting

The most common type of haunting is a residual haunting. This type of haunting may not have anything to do with ghosts! Somehow, energy of the past has been absorbed into the building materials or locations to be replayed over and over again in another time like a video tape. These apparitions often occur because of a change in barometric pressure or temperature which causes energy to expand. A good example of this type of haunting, and a very good chance of your seeing a phantom, is the historic ghost town of Fayette in the Upper Peninsula at the tip of the Garden Peninsula.

It was once one of the UP's most productive iron-smelting operations that became home to over five hundred residents, most were immigrants from Canada, Britain, and northern Europe. It remained in operation from 1867–1891, long enough to impact its energy into the dolomite bluffs and limestone quarries that shelter the small village from the north winds. Limestone is a well-known conductor of energy as is underground water; both are present in Fayette, so is it any wonder that visitors to the park report seeing "ghosts?"

The most recent occurrence of a sighting of the paranormal took place this past summer as a woman and her husband were touring the company store. It had burned down a long time ago, and the new one was built of limestone. They had no idea of what they were about to encounter as they walked through the building. As they went into a room resembling an office, they stopped short as they watched a man who seemed to be putting things on a shelf, but there was no shelf and no items in his hands—only the man, wearing dark brown pants and a white shirt, putting things in proper order. They, at first, thought he was a mime, but as they watched he slowly disappeared. They discovered after talking with one of park personnel that he has been seen in that same place through the years making the same repetitive motions. A woman from Escanaba who is the owner of a popular restaurant there told the story of her visit when she watched a pregnant woman dressed in black wearing a black bonnet walk the length of the manager's porch only to disappear into a white mist. In telling her story, she was informed that a pregnant wife of a former mill manager died in childbirth in the house. Visitors often inquire why they hear the clanking of what sounds like water pipes coming from vacant buildings or the sounds of metal hitting metal and the sound of engines in different areas? A change in barometric pressure seems to cause an increase in this type of activity.

Just before a thunderstorm engulfed the park, a woman and her friend who had visited the Curtis Art Show earlier that day took a step into the furnace building. They immediately saw a man with a big moustache of that time period near the furnace in the back of the room yelling very loudly. He was not yelling at her and her friend but at what seemed towards laborers amongst a deafening din of intense activity. It ended in a moment, but what they encountered that day was a psychic flash into that time and place. The dolomite bluffs could very well have held the intense expanded energy captive in that factory.

As you can see, the residual haunting is quite unlike an intelligent haunting where the spirits seem to interact with you. The Battle of Gettysburg is the most famous of residual hauntings where guns, hoof beats, and shadows of soldiers can be witnessed by the unwary tourist. Old castles seem to be imprinted with residual spirits. But remember, they are just pictures, as if in a film; these sightings occur in places where energy of the period seems to be trapped and the spirits involved have no idea you are watching them nor do they care.

Chapter 8

The Paulding Light Revisited

Viewing location for the Paulding Light on Robbins Pond Road

f or those readers that have read this account in *A Ghostly Road Tour of Michigan's Upper Peninsula,* it has been shortened from the original. The story is repeated here as new information has come to light regarding this mystery.

This phenomenon is located off US-45, just four miles north of Watersmeet. You need to turn on Robbins Pond Road and follow the gravel road to a large boulder and a barricade. Both prevent further travel to the valley below. Try to arrive about twenty minutes before twilight. As it appears on a regular basis, but not always at the same time, you will encounter cars lining up on both sides of the road and people standing in small groups watching and waiting. And then, there it is! A distant spark on the horizon growing larger and larger, coming closer and closer. Then slowly, as if burning out, it disappears.

After a short wait, the lights reappear, two this time, dancing, it seems, along the power line that stretches into the distant hills. Impossible, your brain will tell you. The lights travel to the small creek below then seem to squeeze together into one and slowly recede into the distance.

Often called ghostlights, will-o'-the-wisps, spooklights, and earthlights, they generally appear in the south and western United States. Usually described as a glowing ball or balls of light, they often appear in every color of the rainbow. They are often said to exhibit bizarre behaviors, such as vanishing or

The Paulding Light

splitting in two when something approaches them too closely. They usually appear in a fixed location and appear at set times such as twilight or sunset, but they rarely appear in rain, snow, or fog.

There are many theories and legends surrounding these mysterious lights. Some attempts at explaining the lights include reflections from nearby traffic, low planes, gas from nearby marsh lands, or ghosts. Common folktales from the locals include the tale of the spirit of an old railroad brakeman swinging his lantern, an Indian spirit searching for his war club, a UFO, or Pancake Joe dancing on the power line in protest to the power company running lines across his property. The lights have been reported here since the turn of the century, long before the power company.

On August 12, 2010, *Fact or Faked: Paranormal Files*, a SyFy TV series, aired an investigation by team members hoping to solve the mystery of the Paulding Light. The team members included: Bill, lead scientist; Joel, journalist; Ben, former FBI agent; Larry, special effects specialist; Chu Lan, photography expert; and Austin, a stunt expert.

Upon arriving at the site, they waited in anticipation for the light to appear, and appear it did. Its appearance astonished the team. They spent the rest of that night's encounter interviewing people at the site and then planned their strategy for a solution to the mystery light.

Having heard the legend of the ghost of the railroad brakeman from locals and other legends, they would also try to debunk the popular belief by locals that it was caused by headlights from cars on a nearby highway or that the lights may be from small planes from an isolated nearby airport. They also had to take into consideration radioactivity and combustible gases, that is, swamp gas.

They first used a four wheeler to locate the point of origin of the light. Once the light had been spotted, team members in the field were notified by radio of the coordinates. To their amazement, although standing directly under where the light should be, there was no visual contact whatsoever. None. The team in the field tried several immediate locations but saw nothing.

They next tried to locate radioactivity in the area and once again found nothing. The needle didn't move. The reading was a straight line nothing. They searched for combustible gases with their equipment and again found nothing. The high-tech instruments in use that night recorded nothing unusual.

Their third attempt involved having the police block both ends of a nearby highway for a time while they tried to imitate the light with their car headlights. They used both high and low beams. They also tried their hazard lights. Then they tried the test with a 4x4 truck. The team below at the Robbins Pond Road location saw nothing in all of the tests on the highway. Spectators that evening also reported not seeing any lights at the time of the tests. Not giving up, they tried flying a plane directly over the area while a team member held a 25-million candle power light. The pilot followed a laser beam coordinated by team members on the ground. It lined up with the path of the Paulding Light. Although similar, this light was not low enough, and the sound of the plane's engine could be plainly heard.

They had one last idea. It involved ghost hunting. They decided to do some EVP work at the site of origin. This experiment also failed. There was no conclusive evidence recorded.

The team concluded that the Paulding Light is an unidentifiable natural occurrence and it remains a mystery. Now, most Yoopers already knew this and could have saved the SyFy channel a lot of money.

Chapter 9

Sweet Dreams Inn
VictorianBed and
Breakfast

*S*hould you decide to spend a night, you will have more than sweet dreams at the Sweet Dreams Inn, which was built as a family home by William Wallace in 1890 in Bay Port, Michigan. William Wallace was born September 12, 1862, in nearby Port Hope. He became a well-known businessman throughout Michigan's Thumb area. By 1915, he was the majority stockholder in the Bay Port Fish Company, and at that time Saginaw Bay was rated as having the largest fresh water fisheries in the world. Tourists also came on excursions to Bay Port from the cities to a stone quarry located a few miles outside the village for rock hunting; it was not long before the quarry became the Wallace Stone Company and Quarry. It was purchased in 1890 by Wallace and remains in operation to this day.

In that same year, he built the rambling family home overlooking Lake Huron. Having three stories, the living quarters were located on the first and second floors while a wooden-floored ballroom stretched across the third floor. Because of its wonderful views of Wildfowl Bay from its third floor windows, the ballroom became Wallace's favorite place to smoke a cigar and leave the bustle of the household.

William and his first wife, Francis, were the parents of five children. Not long after her death from a staph infection following the birth of her last child, he married for the second time and soon another child was added to the family brood—a girl. Her name was Ora.

At the present time, the Wallace's former home, known as the Sweet Dreams Inn, has a history of tragic deaths and ghosts. The house is a labyrinth of secret passageways, twisting hallways and winding staircases, informal and formal parlors, fireplaces, maid's quarters, dining and breakfast rooms, countless closets that create puzzles of doorways, and seven bedrooms.

The haunting sounds of the Wallace children playing are heard echoing in the maze of rooms and hallways. Doorknobs wiggle, lights turn on and off, widows open and close, and doors slam; children's laughter rings throughout the house from top to bottom. Most frequently, they are heard during the eternally long Michigan winter nights. The present owner often senses the presence of Mr. Wallace, especially in the ballroom; Wallace was very proud of the ballroom. The owner has caught glimpses of him as he passes from one room to another on the third floor. He is rather shorter then she thought he would be. More times then she would like, she has felt icy tendrils of cold wrap around her legs as she enters the third floor to clean after guests have departed. She does not like to be up there alone.

Ora, the youngest child of Wallace and the only child of his second wife, has become a familiar spirit in the house. She often appears in the third floor windows overlooking the driveway. She sporadically appears in different rooms, but the Peacock Room remains her favorite, perhaps because she loved the color blue and wore it frequently. Somewhat of a tease, her presence is often betrayed by the sudden disappearance of an object and its reappearance several hours later or the sudden movement caught from the corner of your eye of a lamp or a book. The furnace cannot heat the rooms where Ora has decided to spend the day… or night.

Sweet Dreams Inn

It was late September, a time after tourists had returned to the city leaving the village of Bay Port resting in the soft, quiet autumn days, when two delightful ladies from Harbor Beach decided to spend a night at the Sweet Dreams Inn after reading of the haunting in their local newspaper. They giggled their way to Bay Port as they followed the lakeshore on M-25 up and around the Thumb. They reassured each other that, although they were willing to be scared, they were also somewhat nervous of what they might encounter that evening.

It was raining that late fall afternoon as they pulled into the driveway of the inn. A chill spread through Millie as she looked up at the house. She glanced over at Pat, who had stopped the car at the bottom of the drive, and asked, "Is it pink? Or is it purple?"

"In this rain, who can tell?" Pat replied.

"It certainly looks spooky," replied Millie as Pat parked the car. They walked up the wooden steps to the porch where the owner greeted them with a smile and opened the front door.

"Welcome to Sweet Dreams, ladies. Follow me and I will show you to your room. It's upstairs on the second floor." They followed her through a darkened dining room (It was so dark, was it a dining room?) to a narrow stairway with a shaky handrail. Turning left at the top of the thirteen steps—Millie counted them—they followed their hostess down a long, narrow hallway to a door where a brass plate identified it as the Peacock Room.

"Here we are, ladies," she said as she opened the door... this is the most haunted room in the house. Breakfast is 7:00 to 9:00 AM. Homemade blueberry coffee cake, juice, and, of course, fresh coffee. Check out is 11:00—that is..." she laughed as she turned to look back them as she reentered the hallway, "...if you spend the whole night. Oh, almost forgot, there are no keys for the rooms. Just fasten the door with this hook and eye for privacy," she added as she pointed to the small hook on the door. "Any questions?" After explaining that the Bay Port Inn down the road served meals, she left them standing and staring at each other in the blue wallpapered room.

"Thus, the fun begins," said Pat.

Millie placed her overnight bag on the small stand next to the dresser while Pat grabbed her camera case saying, "Let's go, Millie. Let's take some pictures and check out the town." They stepped into the long, shadowed hallway to find their hostess at the end quietly standing with her arms folded in the darkened landing by the stairwell.

"Hello, ladies, anything I can help you with?" she inquired quietly.

"Just heading out to take some pictures," answered Pat. They made their way downstairs, past the silent kitchen and dining room to the front door.

"God, that was spooky," whispered Millie.

"What in the devil was she doing just standing there?" asked Pat.

"The only ghost I have seen so far is her," Millie answered.

Pat took pictures from all angles as they made their way around the perimeter of the house and then on to the Bay Port Inn. The rain slowed to a mist as they finished dinner and made their way back to the inn. Silence surrounded their return. Going up the stairway, they heard heavy footsteps ahead of them as they made their way to the Peacock Room. "There must be another guest staying here tonight," murmured Pat.

"Sounds like a man's footsteps, but it sounds like he went up to the third floor." Millie said.

Entering their room, they heard the footsteps above them, pacing back and forth. "There's nothing up there, is there? I mean, I thought the rooms up there were vacant because they are redoing them or something?" questioned Pat.

"Well, someone is up there now," answered Millie. "Maybe they are checking for leaks in the roof or something. You know how these old places are."

As they prepared for bed, they suddenly stopped what they were doing and gave each other puzzled looks as they listened to the distant sounds... was it children? Were they running up and down the hallway?

"You hear them too?" Millie asked.

"Shush." whispered Pat.

They quietly inched the door open to investigate the haunting sounds. The hallway was empty. Shadows played on the walls cast by light from the heavy, metal sconces. They walked over to the stairs only to look down at the black void in which nothing moved. Pat had shivers run up her back as they returned to their room, shaken but determined to enjoy their stay and willing to be scared. Millie recalled the story their hostess had recounted of the sounds of children running and playing in the halls, the ghosts of William Wallace's children, she maintained.

Millie shivered as they re-entered the room. Unwilling to admit to themselves that the ghosts of kids were playing in the hallway, Pat slipped into the blue-covered bed and prepared to read a chapter in *A Ghostly Road Tour* while Mille searched the closet for another blanket. The room had turned downright frigid since the sun had set. Blanket in hand, she heard Pat cry out, "Help! Millie!"

Dropping the blanket, Millie fought her way out of the closet to find Pat with her back pushed up against the door. "What's wrong?" Millie cried.

"The door! Someone is trying to get in! I watched the knob turn and then the door started to rattle! I actually saw the hook lift up off the eye. Help me keep it closed! It keeps pushing me!"

"Get out of the way, Pat," Millie ordered as she shoved Pat aside and flung the door open. There was nothing there but the sound of footsteps retreating down the hall. Soft music floated from the third floor; they had no inclination to discover its source.

Millie closed the door and forced the back of desk chair under the doorknob. "There, nothing is going to get in here now. Besides, isn't this we came for… to see ghosts?"

"Some ghost hunters we are," mumbled Pat. "I don't mind seeing them, but I sure don't like hearing them. Besides, I don't even believe in them."

Millie went back to the closet to retrieve the blanket she had dropped on the closet floor. It was no longer there. She looked around the room and saw it lying on top of the desk. She was not surprised. Great, she thought to herself, now we have got ourselves a haunted blanket. She spread it over the bed just as Pat remarked, "Look, it's so cold in here I can see my breath!" Trying to forget how cold the room had gotten, they recalled the newspaper article written about the investigation of the inn. The team leader had heard and tape-recorded footsteps walking around the very bed they were going to try to sleep in for the night. He reported the footsteps had walked from one side of the bed to the other several times as if deciding whether to climb in. They waited to hear the same sound of footsteps, but only the sound of a slow waltz drifted down from the third floor ballroom through the rooms and hallways as they fell into a restless sleep.

The following morning found Millie and Pat gathering their belongings. As they walked down the hall to the staircase, there was a young girl of about eleven or twelve standing at the landing. She smiled and then turned and disappeared through the door that led to the third floor. "Did you see that, Pat?"

"I saw nothing and neither did you."

"What about breakfast? Aren't we going to stay for breakfast?" asked Mille.

Pat replied, "I could use a cup of hot coffee, but I am not willing to see what serves us. Are you?" The sounds of music followed them as they left the house. The misty apparitions of Mr. Wallace and a young Ora watched their progress through the third floor window that overlooks the driveway.

Mr. Wallace, Ora, and several of the children remain at the Sweet Dreams Inn while their souls search for eternity.

It started to rain again.

Chapter 10

The Haunting of the Loop-Harrison Mansion

The Loop-Harrison mansion is located in Port Sanilac on M-25 in Michigan's Thumb. Doctor Joseph Loop and his lovely wife, Jane Gardner, built the Second Empire style mansion of yellow brick that was barged across the lake from Ontario, Canada. They settled into the mansion in 1875. With three floors, twenty rooms, and a summer kitchen, Jane had her work cut out for her in choosing the special pieces that would decorate the home. Most of the items she and her husband purchased during that time remain in the mansion today. Each room creates a perfect image of life in the mid-1800s to the early 1900s. The floors gleam, the chandeliers sparkle, the tables and cupboards shine with wax, and the sofas and chairs seem to wait for Jane, the doctor, or perhaps Ada to return.

The doctor kept his office, surgery, and waiting room on the first floor where the smells of medicinals and herbs grown and collected by Jane still linger. He serviced a forty-mile circuit in all kinds of weather on horseback and buggy. The couple had only one child, Ada, who together with her mother and father soon became well known throughout the area for their kindness and good works to all who needed help.

Ada was twenty-one by the time they moved into the mansion. She soon left home to attend a female seminary in Ann Arbor. After graduation she became a teacher and taught school in Pontiac for two years. It was during this time that she met her husband, the Reverend Julius Harrison. They

The Loop-Harrison Mansion is located in Port Sanilac, Michigan.

returned to the mansion to live with her parents while Julius traveled around the Thumb visiting his pastorals. Being a Projectionist,* he was a popular speaker as he supported the Women's Christian Temperance Union, a fact Doctor Loop did not appreciate. Ada gave birth to two sons, Stanley and Fred, both handsome boys who grew up in the mansion that Ada inherited after the death of her parents. Stanley became a captain sailing the Great Lakes, and Fred followed his grandfather's footsteps and became a doctor and settled in Pennsylvania.

Ada lived all but twelve years of her life in her parent's home. She loved the mansion and the people of the area. Her Steinway piano was brought by boat to the pier in Port Sanilac and hauled by wagon up the hill to the mansion. She played frequently and gave lessons to people of the village

---

* Projectionist is an early term used in a pastoral manner—to project ourselves forward to see where our present behavior is taking us.

*Ada's bedroom where her spirit was seen
floating about a foot off the floor.*

patiently smiling at their mistakes. She continued her parent's philanthropy and became a prominent and beloved member of the community. She also became a ghost.

She loved to walk the shore of Lake Huron, and she was often seen gazing out to the lake, enjoying its many moods. In 1925 she walked down to the shoreline to watch a storm cross the lake. Winds tugged at her long skirts as she pulled her cape closer about her shoulders. She made her way up the hill to where she could see the lights of the mansion between the stinging raindrops. Thunder drowned out all the sound as she began to cross the muddy road (today it is M-25). Carelessly driving without headlights, a Model T automobile struck her. She was carried from the side of the road up the steps of the home she loved, and there she died.

Today, visitors to the mansion report seeing Ada gliding through the halls and catch glimpses of her as she sits at her piano. Listen carefully as you walk through the home for the sound of soft piano music drifting down the stairway and though the halls. Recently, a young man was to install smoke alarms throughout the home. Standing on a ladder outside of Ada's second floor bedroom, he paused thinking he heard a noise from Ada's room. He turned to see her apparition wearing a long white dress. She was floating about a foot off the floor while gazing out the window facing the lake. Needless to say, he left in a hurry.

Motorists driving along M-25 on a rainy stormy days or nights often find themselves watching a woman with a long dress and cape trying to cross the highway. Just as they reach her, she disappears in the mist. Some have reported they catch a glimpse of her in their rear view mirror as they pass the front of the mansion.

The window where the spirit of Stanley has been seen peering through the curtains at the herb garden.

She was fond of her parent's herb garden and has been reported strolling near it wearing a bonnet and carrying an umbrella. Her son Stanley's apparition has been seen in his second floor bedroom window peering through the curtains overlooking the herb garden. Whispers, items being moved on their own, books falling from their shelves, cupboard doors opening and closing by invisible hands, and the laughter of small boys and their running footsteps are just a few examples of the paranormal activity that take place in the mansion. It's a lovely home and is haunted by lovely spirits.

There is nothing to fear at the Loop-Harrison mansion except, perhaps, on a rainy day?

Chapter 11

Ghosts of Forester Inn

The Forester Inn squats like a neon frog on the shoulder of M-25 about thirty-eight miles north of Port Huron. Tendrils of fog slip up the clapboard siding and wind through the porch posts beckoning possible passersby to stop in for a beer or burger. The dark entry is punctuated by deer heads, lottery machines and advertising signs. Knotty pine walls are accentuated by the server's uniforms of blue jeans and new balance tennis shoes. The bar stretches along the left inviting you to sit and hear a story or two from Don about the ghosts that inhabit the inn. The smell of fried fish drifts from the kitchen. It doesn't look spooky or creepy, but then again, it's not always how it looks; it's what lingers after the customers have gone—and it's not the smell of fish or burgers we are talking about!

Across the street is the abandoned Quay house, the original home of the family of the legendary Minnie Quay whose spirit reportedly follows the shoreline and lingers near the family headstone in the cemetery. Perhaps hers is the apparition with golden hair and a flowing white gown often observed standing by the end of the long bar in the darkened room. Sailors say if you taste the salty tears of your love before you sail, she will remain faithful until your return. Indeed, the spirit of Minnie has remained faithful, even after her death and the death of the sailor she loved.

There are many ghosts wandering throughout the building of the Forester Inn. Don, the bartender, has

witnessed paranormal activity for several years. One especially frightening event took place just as he was closing up one evening. He went into the back room to put away a large kettle when he thought he heard a woman's voice call his name. "Don," it called softly. He stood and listened. He hesitated for a moment and then turned and walked back into the bar expecting to see someone looking for him. Suddenly, a huge crash from the room he had just left shook the floor and echoed throughout the building. He quickly returned to the back room to find a large stainless steel shelf that held an industrial microwave oven, which weighed at least a hundred pounds, had fallen onto the floor. Had someone or something not called his name, he would have been seriously injured.

The basement of the inn is not a place you want to enter alone. Don has been in the cooler there when the door has slammed shut. He has watched dark shadows dart from even darker corners down there. He often feels a female presence in the building. Is it Minnie Quay? Is it her light footsteps he hears on stairs to the lower floor while he is there retrieving supplies? Many nights Don and his staff have heard heavy

Area where the heavy shelf fell; lucky the bartender had been warned.

footsteps pacing the length of the barroom ceiling above them. Nearly all of the help at one time or another have encountered cold spots that are not due to the winter winds. Even customers have complained of the icy cold that grabs their ankles as they enjoy the inn's great pizza.

Knives have gone missing; pots and pans move about on their own; lights go on and off; the scent of lavender perfume displaces the smell of burger and fries. The fan over the salad bar stops, starts, increases its speed, then finely settles down and behaves like a fan should. The hallway to the restrooms is always busy with the supernatural—doors open, toilets flush, the water turns on and off. All are signs of paranormal activity at the inn. One wonders how many ghosts are there here that spend their days and nights searching for eternity?

Have a pizza, enjoy a cold beer and the atmosphere of the Forester Inn. Don't be surprised if a chair moves on its own or if your hands get icy cold as you wait for your beer. Don will explain; it happens all the time.

Chapter 12

The Myth of Minnie Quay

Minnie walked along the sandy shoreline that spring morning as dark clouds lined with gold rose like mountains over Lake Huron. She often followed this path along the shore and took a short-cut through the cemetery to return home after a relaxing stroll. Along her way she passed the small pier that jutted into the lake for ships loading lumber for the down-river ports. This morning there was a ship anchored in the inlet. A small boat with three men made its way to shore.

Minnie stood and watched its progress little knowing her destiny was approaching. She clung to her bonnet as a gust of morning wind pushed at her yellow dress, as if warning her. The skiff landed and the men walked up the sand towards her. They smiled at her and tipped their hats as they passed, but one, the youngest of the group, stopped. He was tall and handsome in his heavy black sweater and baggy pants. She shyly looked into the bluest eyes she had ever seen... and fell in love.

For a year, all through the season when ships could sail the lakes without the danger of ice and northern gale-driven winds, the two would meet, secretly each time the ship stopped at the small port. Minnie's parents refused to allow the beautiful young woman to waste herself on a man without proper means who might never return.

*The abandoned home of Minnie Quay's family
sits across the highway from the Forester Inn.*

Deeply in love with Minnie, the young man promised her they would marry after the long winter had passed. During that winter's lay-up, he returned to Ohio to sell his home and a hotel he had purchased with his earnings as a sailor. He planned to build Minnie a home and purchase the village hotel that he was pleased to see for sale on his last trip to Forester. He would show Minnie's parents he was fully able to support their daughter.

The shipping season began in the early spring when the ice was no longer a danger on the lakes. The young man sailed with his ship all that season until the winds of November warned once again of the dangers of the lakes. The ship picked up a last load of lumber at Alpena and started its journey south. He thought of his Minnie and counted the days when

Quay's family tomestone.

he would see her again. He stood on deck watching the wind pushing clouds, feeling the spray of water on his face as he planned how to approach Minnie's parents with his proposal. As happens in November on the Great Lakes, the ship encountered devastating winds near Port Austin. It was lost with all men on board. The winds that caused the loss of the ship brought over two feet of snow to Minnie's small village; it took a full week for Minnie to hear of the loss of the ship and the man she loved. Devastated, she walked into the cold waters of her destiny. She has never been found or seen again... or has she?

Is she an earthbound spirit tied here in search of her lost love? Is that her spirit walking the shoreline in the early morning as the golden sunrise touches the clouded horizon? Or, could that be Minnie walking along the highway that used to be the dirt road leading to the cemetery?

Mementos left by visitors to the grave of Minnie Quay.

You may visit the Quay tombstone at the Forester Cemetery. Her name, Minnie Quay, is on the lower left side. You will notice how the surface of the tombstone is covered with pennies and various items left by superstitious visitors. As it is said, if you do not leave a memento of your visit, Minnie will follow you home. Many visitors have reported seeing the spirit of Minnie wearing a white bonnet rimmed in black and a long white dress walking in the cemetery and along the shoreline.

Note from the author: I have been informed of a trunk that had been found in the attic of the Quay home that held baby shoes, a Bible, handkerchiefs, and a white bonnet with black ribbons. A previous owner insists the trunk was haunted and it brought bad luck to those who have it in their possession. It is believed to have belonged to the Quay family.

Minnie Quay
1860–1876

Chapter 13

Point aux Barques Lighthouse

*L*ocated between Harbor Beach and Port Austin, the Pointe aux Barques Lighthouse has been watching over the turn to Saginaw Bay for over 163 years. The light is also referred to as "Point of Arks" as a result of ships encountering the shallow shoals and reefs that lurk beneath the dark blue waters extending out into Lake Huron for approximately two miles; this is the "Graveyard of Lake Huron." In November of 1966, a horrific storm would once again bring tragedy to the shores of the lighthouse. The storms of November arrived in the upper lakes with driving gale-force winds of ice and snow that whipped the lake into frenzy with seas of twenty to twenty-five feet.

The *Daniel J. Morrell's* captain was in communication with the freighter *Edward Y. Townsend* while passing Harbor Beach. Both skippers were having a difficult time holding course. They discussed turning around to reach safety in Port Huron but knew they could be caught in a trough between the huge thundering waves. The only remaining possibility was to make an attempt to anchor in the protected waters of Thunder Bay, Ontario. The *Morrell* would never reach that safe haven. She broke so quickly twenty miles north-northeast of the Thumb that a Mayday signal went unsent. Twenty-nine lives were lost that November 29th of 1966.

Today the lighthouse stands serene in the twilight of a summer evening, but beneath her calm exterior, there is a

Point aux Barques Lighthouse

degree of darkness. The remains of many of the victims' bodies of that tragic night in 1966 were found on the shores beneath the lighthouse. Is it possible that on arriving here their spirits stayed? Did they climb the tower to search for their shipmates in the storm? Do their spirits remain locked behind these walls; their sadness lingering for generations?

Anna is the director of the lighthouse and park. She spends the months of the tourist season at the lighthouse and, of course, is very familiar with all of its creaks and groans. There are times when she knows she is not the only one present in the keeper's house; today her eyes follow the sound of heavy footsteps across the gift shop's ceiling. It is nearly dark and time for her to leave and walk across the yard to the assistant keeper's cottage where she has been spending the night during this year's season. She moved to the assistant keeper's cottage because of the increasing reports by tourists during last summer's season of seeing a woman's face with an 1800's hairdo appearing in some mirrors in the keeper's house. Several reported seeing an apparition of a man wearing a life jacket climbing the stairs to the light tower. The sound of heavy footsteps in the hallway tunnel leading to the tower could account for the tendrils of cold air she often felt as she climbed the tower steps. She had had enough. She was beginning to feel uneasy during the daylight hours much less spending another night in the second floor bedroom where just yesterday she found her clothes strewn all over the floor. She did not believe in ghosts, but she was afraid of them.

Shadows grew longer as the sun began to set. She locked the door of the lighthouse behind her and made her way across the yard that separated the two buildings. As she walked, she glanced up at the second floor windows that overlooked the yard. A member of the historical society told her he had seen a woman in the second window to the left when he knew the house was vacant. This evening there was nothing in the window but the reflection of the trees. She took a deep breath as she opened the front door into the hallway.

The cottage atmosphere, unlike the lighthouse residence, was warm and welcoming. She had always felt that the first woman lighthouse keeper, Catherine Shook, the mother of eight children, occasionally returned from the grave to make sure everything is being taken care of in her early home. Anna's disbelief in ghosts had nothing to do with this feeling. Perhaps, she thought to herself, it was Catherine that Mike had seen in the upstairs window.

As in all good ghost stories, it was that time of year when thunderstorms approach the Thumb from the southwest and cause havoc along the shoreline communities. It was one of those nights. Anna warmed the casserole her mother, Sharon, had brought up to the lighthouse that morning. As she made

The tunnel to the light tower.

coffee, lightning lit up the corners of the room and shot across the hallway. While waiting for dinner to be ready, she climbed the stairs to the second floor where her bedroom was the first door at the top of the steps. She was startled to see the windows all closed. She remembered opening them earlier in the day because of the oppressive heat, but there they were, all nicely closed and the curtains tightly pulled keeping the lightning out.

She recalled a conversation with Seul Choix Point Lighthouse tourist guides—most ghosts do not like spring cleaning. She reminded herself that the members of the lighthouse's historical group had been cleaning in and out of the buildings all week and were more than likely responsible for the windows. She hung up her work clothes and pulled on a pair of sweats. She noticed the rugs were clean and the wooden floors shinned with a new coat of wax. She returned to the kitchen. She closed the basement door as she passed,

The assistant keeper's cottage living room.

knowing it often opened and closed of its own accord. No accounting for that.

The coffee smelled good, and the casserole looked done too. She placed her loaded dinner plate, homemade bread from Al's Restaurant, and coffee on a wooden tray and went into the living room to relax in front of the TV.

Thunder rolled across the lake bringing a strong wind with it. She could hear the waves pushing against the shoreline. "I am glad I am not out in this," she said out loud, stuffing another piece of bread into her mouth.

Stairway to the bedrooms in the captain's quarters.

Finishing her dinner, she walked back into the kitchen, past the basement door, which was open—again—and cleaned her dishes and the mess. Just as she was about to walk into the living room, the lights went out. Pitch black. She was quite used to this. She returned to the kitchen for candles and the lantern. The storm was slowly making its way northeast leaving behind the sound of soft raindrops on the porch roof and... the sound of footsteps on the stairs.

Lightning flickered across the hallway floor as she walked to the bottom of the stairway. She watched the flashlight beam climb the stairs to find nothing but darkness there.

Walking back into the living room, she was about to place the lantern down when the lights came back on. Good, she thought, now I can watch TV for a while. Walking back to the kitchen to return the lantern to the cupboard, she once again closed the basement door. She then returned to the living room. Moments later, after getting comfortable on the couch and wrapping herself in her favorite blanket, the TV shut itself off then turned on again—erratic lines filled the screen. She pulled the blanket closer to her chin as she watched in horror as a dark shadow moved from the kitchen hall doorway across the room in front of her. Then, blocking the light from the TV screen, it moved into the front hallway, dimming the light there as it passed. She heard soft footsteps climbing the stairs. It's just Catherine, she thought to herself. I know it's only Catherine. Frigid air stung her face as she took some deep breaths and gathered her courage. She walked into the kitchen noting that the basement door was closed. She grabbed her jacket from the back door hook and left the cottage. That's enough for one night, she said to the car as she drove down the lighthouse road back to Harbor Beach. Checking the time, 11:30 PM, she knew her mother would be up watching a movie. This is one of those times when a girl really needs her mother.

Several months later, Anna gave permission to a paranormal group to investigate the lighthouse. Due to the season opening in a few weeks, an investigation of the assistant keeper's cottage would have to wait until after Labor Day. Loaded with equipment, the team set up cameras in every room and spent the night searching for signs of the paranormal.

The stairway in the assistant lighthouse keeper's cottage where the shadow spirit's footsteps were heard climbing the steps.

After two nights of intensive investigation, it would take the team time to examine the results of their work. Several weeks later, the team leader reported their findings to Anna.

"Is it haunted?" Anna asked.

"During the investigation, we constantly heard the sounds of voices coming from the tower. Although we climbed to the tower several times during that night when we heard the voices, we found nothing there," he replied.

"Footsteps, did you hear any footsteps?" asked Anna.

"The spirits in this place are constantly on the move. We recorded the sound of footsteps in the tower hallway, also in the upstairs, almost like pacing. When we were upstairs, the sounds of movement could be heard coming from downstairs."

Anna sighed, "So it is haunted. The rumors are true."

"You definitely have paranormal activity here at the lighthouse," he replied.

Anna watched the team drive away as she walked back to the lighthouse quarters to make sure all was secure. Prickly cold climbed up her back as she walked into the old kitchen. She caught her breath as she thought she saw a shadow dart through the dining room doorway toward the gift shop. She immediately turned herself around and walked back out the door thinking to herself... the volunteer tour guides will be here any minute... I need a cup of coffee.

Chapter 14

Mary Wilkenson: A Haunting

Aunt Mary Wilkenson

*M*ary Wilkenson sat in her favorite rocking chair in the parlor. The sun had long since departed, leaving the room with shadows slightly moving on the walls caused by the low burning embers in the fireplace. She reread her favorite Emerson passage and smiled to herself as she thought of how surprised her niece would be when she told her of her discovery when she came to visit later that week.

Her niece Emma found her later that week, in the parlor sitting in her favorite rocking chair. She was starting to stink. Her vacant blue eyes stared at the heavy lace drapes across the room. A faint smile still lingered on her cold lips; the rocking chair continued in a meager motion, so slight that you had to look twice to make sure. The book that her aunt had held had slipped to the floor, open to one of the pages of Ralph Waldo Emerson's diverse works:

> "It is the secret of the world that all things subsist and do not die, but retire from sight and afterwards return again nothing is dead; men feign themselves dead, and endure mock funerals and mournful obituaries, and there they stand looking out of the window, sound and well, in some new and strange disguise."

Reading the words, Emma wondered at their meaning. She remembered her great-aunt with sadness. Emma had made an effort to visit her aunt at least once a month. In recent years, her aunt had become a recluse who left the old mansion once a year to travel to England where she collected the various artifacts that littered the house.

Emma called for the ambulance.

They buried her on a stormy fall morning. The darkened sky left no shadows at the gravesite. The few mourners quickly dissolved into the misty rain leaving her standing by the pile of damp earth. Emma, a tall, slender blonde, worked part-time as a dispatcher for the Huron County Sheriff's Department where her fiancé was a deputy. She had recently opened her own restaurant in Port Sanilac, a small village in the Thumb that had become a popular tourist stop. The restaurant, her pride and joy, had been a dream of Emma's for a long time. She redecorated and renamed it The Café, where she served summer guests a selection of specialty sandwiches and salads.

She held the book of Emerson's works tightly in her hand as she bent over to place a small bunch of gold chrysanthemums on the grave. There was no money for a head stone. That would come later.

As Emma wound her way through the small trail between gravestones, she paused to look back; the only spot of color in the bleak cemetery was her bouquet of flowers.

Because Mary Wilkenson had died alone, the Medical Examiner had ordered an autopsy that determined her death was the result of heart failure. Having died intestate succession, Emma inherited the house, its contents, and Aunt Mary's belongings.

Several months after the funeral, when winter just dipped its icy fingers into Michigan's Thumb, she drove northeast a few miles along the shore road to the old Victorian.

It was a house built in the late 1800s typical of its time period. It stood alone, with only a twisting gravel road leading to the house. Standing tall on a slight rise with an aged apple

A likeness of the Wilkenson home.

orchard in the back of the house, it overlooked Lake Huron. It was a large house with a porch that wrapped itself around the entire front exterior. Snow-covered overgrown vines, shrubs, and weeds partially hid the wrought-iron fence that surrounded the property. The gate swung easily as Emma walked up the ice-clad path that led to the main entrance. She took out the key that fit nicely into the locked front door and opened it with ease.

The house had been empty now for over five months. She entered cautiously. The musty odor of disuse overwhelmed her as she made her way through the long hall, passing a dead dusty fern on the large stairway post. Frigid air smothered her. She shivered and pushed her hands into the pockets of her navy blue pea coat. The dark wooden floors creaked as she made her way into the parlor filled with furniture of a period that did not include the nineteenth century. Something moved near the rocking chair that squatted in front of the fireplace. Of course, she thought, there must be mice, or maybe even a stray cat had found its way in. Her eyes searched the room carefully. The ornate mirror that hung over the fireplace distorted the reflection of the large potted fern on the newel post; it seemed to move as if a wind had caught its dead leafy vines. She quickly turned around to look at it head on; there was no movement. She watched it carefully for a moment, shook her head as if to clear it, and then turned her attention back to the room. The walls were decorated with heavy-framed pictures that included faded country landscapes and several sketches of the lake. Three long, narrow windows that lined the right side of the room were covered with heavy lace draperies; thick with dust, they clung to the ornaments that held them in place. Although it was a sunny day when she entered, only filtered light crept through the draped windows.

She moved into the dining room. Again, a shroud of ice-cold air surrounded her. "God, it is cold in here," she muttered. "And what the hell was that?" she yelped as her peripheral vision caught a movement from the parlor she had just left. Goose bumps ran up her arms to the back of her neck where the hair was standing on end. "Really now, there is nothing here. Nothing. I've let this old place spook me," she said out loud as she noted the eight high-backed chairs that held court around a lengthy table covered with dust. One of the chairs was out of place, as if someone had just gotten up. Another potted fern sat on a pedestal beside a buffet on which a large Bible was centered. Above the buffet was an oval picture of her grandmother wearing a blue dress, with a slight smile teasing her pink lips.

Emma shivered as she remembered the passage from Emerson. Again, goose bumps ran up her legs and down her arms. I don't believe in ghosts, she thought as she continued to look around. Yellowed lace curtains hung in folds across a bay window; more potted ferns sat on the window seat. Her hands were freezing as she moved into the kitchen through a swinging door. A cup of dreary tea was on the wood planked table. A spoon lay upside down next to it; other than that everything was dust covered but orderly. It's warmer in here, she thought. She peaked into the pantry that was the size of a small bedroom. Its shelves were lined with staples: flour, sugar, and tea. Back in the kitchen, she looked toward the door that opened to the back porch. I will need help cleaning out this place, she thought as she went back to the main staircase and began to climb up the carpeted steps. A hand-carved railing led the way up to the hallway. She reached out to turn on the overhead light. She flicked it several times. No lights. Moreover, it was dark and getting darker. You know, I need to lock up my imagination right now, she thought as she glanced over the balcony just in time to see the fern below moving again. What the hell, she thought, is wrong with that damn fern? She momentarily discounted it and opened the door into a blue bedroom, fully furnished with a canopy bed.

It had been years since she had been upstairs in the place, and she remembered fondly the hours she had spent in her younger days of "overnights" at Aunt Mary's. Clouds of dust scattered as she walked to the large closet doors. Few clothes were hung there. The shelves were vacant. She recalled the small door in the back of the closet and had to bend over to open it. Inside was a huge storage area filled to the top with boxes of every size. She walked back through the closet, through the bedroom, and into the hallway, which ended at Aunt Mary's bedroom. The door was located in a small alcove. She opened it and peeked in. The room was large and had a cozy sitting area next to the tall bowed windows that overlooked the orchard and the lake. She remembered her aunt sitting in the large leather chair with her feet propped up on the needlepoint stool watching for the Great Lakes freighters that passed in the distance. She had loved the lake and the ships.

Emma felt her eyes moisten as memories of happier times with her aunt washed over her like gentle waves. She pulled the door behind her as she went slowly down the stairway back to the main floor. She blew at the fern as she passed by. It didn't move. Silly old thing, she thought as she passed by it on her way back to the kitchen door that led to the back porch. It was a lovely porch with a wicker table and two rocking chairs. She fondly recalled the tea parties Aunt Mary had arranged with her three favorite dolls, Aunt Mary, and herself. Even though it was cold out, she sat down into one of the rocking chairs and stretched out, putting her hands behind her head. Well, what do I do? I certainly can't live here; it's much too big. I would love to live here, but it's miles from work. She knew her aunt wanted her to live in the old Victorian. Sadly, she thought, I will have to sell it and all the stuff in it. Aunt Mary hasn't left any money behind. It is a mystery how she lived and kept this old house up. Poor old dear, thought Emma as she pushed herself up from the chair. She looked back at the wicker furniture thinking, I have to get that inside.

As she traveled the shore road to her apartment above the restaurant, she reached Mike on her cell phone. She told him about the house and its contents. "We'll need help, Mike, cleaning it out."

He laughed and told her he had some vacation time built up and he could get some of the other guys from the department to help. "How about we make a plan to do this when the weather gets warmer though; it's too damn cold to do anything this time of year."

"Yeah," she replied, "and we can have an estate sale. I'll give Molly a call to help too. With that antiques shop of hers, this should be right up her alley."

Emma had made friends with Molly when she bought the burger and shake place. Molly owned an antiques store and consignment auction gallery about two buildings down from Emma's. Molly's shop, The Attic, held treasures from all over Huron and Sanilac Counties and a few places beyond their borders. She was shorter than Emma by an inch or so and always wore a baseball cap and blue jeans. Her short black hair framed a sweet face that had never seen make-up.

It was barely 3:30 and already getting dark as she pulled up to the parking lot behind the restaurant; she noticed that Molly's shop had lights on. She picked her way through the shoveled sidewalk and walked in the back door. "Molly, you here?" Emma called.

"Here, in the front," answered Molly.

"I've been to Aunt Mary's. You're going to help me sort through all of the stuff, aren't you?" asked Em as she made her way through assorted furniture and knickknacks.

"All of those antiques?" said Molly as Em spotted her on her knees polishing the legs of an old chair.

"All of them," replied Emma.

"When do I get to go look?" asked Molly.

"This weekend OK?" answered Em.

"Gosh, you bet I will. Try to leave me here," answered Molly breathlessly as she stood up and smiled her "Molly happy smile" at Em.

Emma had the weekend off from her dispatcher duties and Mike had to work, so Molly and Em planned to drive to the Victorian house together to spend the weekend. Mike had told her she needed to turn on the heat and power as a house sitting vacant through the winter months would invite problems, frozen pipes for one. Em had arranged for the utilities. They packed some groceries and headed up the north shore road. It had started to snow and the wind was picking up as they pulled into the portico by the side door.

"Yikes, it's cold in here!" Molly cried as she made her way through the hallway. "Which way to the kitchen?"

"Keep going and make a left at the first opportunity," Em called back.

"What happened to the heat?"

"Maybe it needs to be turned up. I think that thingamajig is in the cellar," she replied as she caught up to Molly in the kitchen.

"Well, the lights are working," answered Molly as the room lit in a soft glow after she found a switch.

"Good, now come with me to the cellar," Em responded as she opened the door that led to the bare bones of the place. She led the way down the wooden steps while Molly switched on the light by pulling on a string overhead. "Boy, it's bleak down here," said Em.

"Yeah, and really spooky. Look, Em, there's the furnace."

"Where?"

"Right in front of you."

"But it's so small."

"That's because it's brand new!" exclaimed Molly.

"But... brand new...where on earth did Aunt Mary get the money for a brand new furnace?"

"Whatever... is it working?"

"Yep, it's humming so it should be getting warm upstairs."

They returned to the kitchen where the heat seemed to be spreading its warm fingers. "So what do we do first?" asked Molly.

"I made a casserole for dinner, so I'll pop that in the oven for an hour. Meanwhile, I'll give you the grand tour."

Em wanted to begin the informal inventory in the huge closet that was behind the blue bedroom as the casserole began its journey to being warmed. They turned on the lights as they started up the long stairway. "Hey Em…"

"Yeah," she answered.

"Why is that fern moving on the newel post?"

"Because, that's what it does," laughed Em as she continued up the stairs.

Molly looked back at it as she followed. "This place is a museum. I cannot believe the beautiful items your aunt has collected! And they seem to be from all time-periods."

"I know. The house is filled from top to bottom. In addition, she loved every thing in here. A lot of the things she brought back with her from England, and others she had shipped. I remember when I was a kid strange packages were delivered, usually at night. I cannot figure out where she got the money for all of this," she said as she waved her arms around the room.

"She probably bought and sold. With all of her trips to Europe, she more than likely had a wide circle of collectors and investors, people of influence in the antiques market. And, from the looks of what I see, she did quite well. You know, Em, when you say your aunt didn't have any money, you're wrong. She has plenty and its all here in this house!"

The contents of the closet proved to be a disappointment as it was discovered to be filled with empty boxes and cartons instead of treasures. They spent the better part of an hour rummaging through the boxes to make sure they hadn't missed anything. Em did find a 16 x 20 portrait of her aunt that stared out at her from a filigreed gold frame. It was terribly old, the frame that is; the picture looked to be very recent. She leaned it against a chest of drawers.

They started back downstairs, passing the fern on the newel post without incident, and went back to the kitchen where the smell of the casserole filled the room. As Em used hot pads to remove the hot dish, Molly set the table in the kitchen, which was warmer and more inviting then the formal dinning room. Em placed the casserole on the table along with a basket of hard rolls just out of the oven.

"Eat, Molly, while it's hot. The coffee should be done in a few minutes."

"These are Fiesta."

"What?"

"The dishes. They are a pattern called Fiesta. These are collectable, and your aunt seems to have a bunch of them mixed in with an assortment of everyday dishes. I'll check them out later. Yum, I love your casseroles, Em. Did you bring butter for the rolls?"

"Yep, on the counter next to the coffee pot. Do you want coffee now? I think it's done."

"Sure. Did you bring cream too?"

"Next to the butter."

"Where?"

"Next to the butter."

"You mean this cream sitting here on the table next to the rolls?"

Emma turned quickly around to face the table. She looked from the counter to the table, looked at Molly, back at the counter and then back to the cream.

"Come on, Molly. I didn't put it there and it was in a half and half carton so stop fooling around."

They both stopped and looked at the small stick-handled blue creamer. Neither said a word.

They continued to finish their meal, and after cleaning up their mess, they walked into the parlor with cups of strong coffee. They sat in front of the fireplace. It was a cozy room in spite of the fact that it was the room in which Emma had found her aunt Mary's body. The wind was coming from the east, across the lake. Ice-cold drafts swirled around their feet bringing shivers up their backs and around their necks.

"God, it is cold in here," said Molly, shivering.

"It's just the wind," replied Emma, "The thermostat next to the hallway says 73. It's got to be the wind off the lake. This time of year it is always frigid." She got up and walked over to peer out the window. Snow danced around the porch and up the steps. It was just a bad winter's night, she thought. No sense in scaring Molly. Em had seen the rocking chair's movement as they had walked into the parlor with their coffee. She ignored it and had purposely sat down in the chair. Move over, she said to herself, whoever you are.

"What time is it? asked Em.

"More coffee time," replied Molly as she walked to the kitchen.

Em, following behind, said, "We should start our inventory tonight. There's nothing else to do. No TV. No radio. Zip. Nada."

"OK by me," answered Molly. "Where do we start, upstairs or down here?"

"Let's start here in the kitchen. Let's find out how much of that…"

"Fiestaware," interrupted Molly.

"…there is," continued Emma.

They counted and recorded in the laptop every piece of dishware in the tall cupboards. "That's the kind of stuff the summer tourists look for," said Molly.

Both tired and more than a little dusty, they agreed it was time to tuck themselves in. Stifling yawns, they climbed the stairs and agreed to share the blue bedroom with the huge bathroom right at the top of the stairs. The wind continued to push against the windows, and snow crept in under the ledge.

Em snuggled into the bed as Molly finished brushing her teeth in the bathroom when a sudden slam brought both of them to the end of the bed.

"What the hell was that?" cried Molly.

"I think it was a door," said Emma.

They both ran into the hall. They looked over the edge of the balcony into the downstairs. Nothing. They both looked down the hall to Aunt Mary's room and the door was closed. However, hadn't it been that way? Was the wind so strong to cause that heavy door to slam? Em walked down the hall and opened Aunt Mary's door. Nothing was changed. Molly followed behind and peered over Em's shoulder and whispered, "I don't see anything, do you?"

"No, because it is just the wind and this is a very old house. Doors close, ferns dance, and Lord knows what else, but it's because this is an old house. So come on, let's get back to bed!" Em said emphatically.

The following morning, after several hours of cataloging items in the dining room, they decided to take a break and retreated to the breakfast room to sip on hot coffee that did little to dispel the icy cold that seemed to spread from the very heart of the house to wrap them up as in a shroud.

Emma became very quiet as she sipped from one of her aunt's English mugs. Quietly, Molly asked, "What is it Em? What is wrong?" She reached out and touched Emma's hand.

"It's Aunt Mary. I am so sad that I didn't spend more time with her these past few years. I feel as though she is still here, Molly… and she doesn't want me to leave."

Molly stood up and walked to the window that overlooked the back garden saying, "I understand, Em. True grief always seems to carry guilt. But, Em, maybe you should rethink your feelings about selling this place. It really is lovely and… there is something here… something…"

Em interrupted, "You mean something like Aunt Mary's spirit? You're right, of course, Molly, but I don't believe in that sort of thing, but I do believe I have to reconsider selling. Let's go back to town. I need to get away from that fern!"

By mid-summer, Emma had decided definitely she could not keep Aunt Mary's home; it was just too far to travel back and forth to her job, and Mike would never move this far from his job. That alone could be the end of any wedding plans she had silently hoped for with him.

She was pleased when Colonel Dave Osentoski of Osentoski Realty Company and Auctioneering from Caro, Michigan, agreed to conduct a public sale of her aunt's estate. During the following weeks, the auction employees would sort through Aunt Mary's lovely treasures and antiques. Emma did not return until the day of the auction. Molly and Mike came with her to watch the proceedings.

The Wilkenson auction.

People flooded the property looking for bargains. She spotted what she believed to be several dealers, probably from the city. Molly and Mike had wandered off to examine the Fiestaware while she walked up the porch steps to sit on the old hanging swing that was partially hidden by thick foliage and climbing roses, a favorite place of hers when she was young. She felt a heavy sadness press down on her as she pushed herself with her foot. She was watching the sunlight flicker through the leaves when she became aware of a gathering of the dappled sunlight forming a shape directly in front of her. The noise of the auction receded into the distance as Aunt Mary's spirit stood in front of her sobbing into a lace handkerchief. Her sobs were broken by her soft, pleading voice, "Please, Em, do not do this. Please." Then the dappled sunshine eased into sunlit rays of floating dust and… she was gone. Stunned, Emma recalled the fern's movements, the disappearing objects, the unaccounted for noises and footsteps; now she knew the reason for them. Aunt Mary was not happy, not at all.

Emma shot from the swing to find Mike and Molly. Dragging them with her to the auctioneer while explaining what had happened, she called a halt to the sale. Dumbfounded, people left, some angry, most puzzled by the unusual events. Soon the estate was vacant, and the only people left were the employees of the auctioneer and Colonel Dave himself. He, too, was mystified by the sudden halt to what was to be one of his largest auctions of the season. An agreement was made to pay for his services. This was not the first time he had encountered paranormal occurrences during his career of auctioneering.

Within the next year, the items that had been sold that day slowly made their way back to Emma. It seems many of the purchases were haunted. Emma was continually amazed at the stories she heard when items from the auction were returned. Rumors of the apparition of an elderly lady dressed

in blue who pleaded with a present owner to return a mirror or bedroom set or a vase. They did. Stories of items floating from one room to another discouraged buyers from keeping their treasures. There were reports of loud banging from whatever room the item or items had been placed. Stories of footsteps and loud groans accompanied many of the items. An apparition of a lady in blue appearing in a dresser mirror and a broach that turned green every time it was worn by its new owner are examples of a haunting of personal possessions. This type of haunting is quite frequent as buyers of flea markets, garage sales, and auction items will tell you.

Mike and Emma were married late that fall. Shortly after moving into the house, she was busy hanging the old painting of the portrait of Aunt Mary that she had found upstairs over the fireplace when it slipped from her hands and fell to the floor. As she brought the broken frame into the kitchen, she could see another painting under it. Curious, she carefully removed the picture of Aunt Mary. She only glimpsed at what lay underneath, but she screamed for Mike. Molly, who was there helping that day, came running from the front parlor. "Look, Molly! Oh my God! Look!" There beneath Mary's smiling face was a Van Gogh. Mike entered the room to stare in amazement at the signature of the artist while Molly and Em ran from the room to tear paintings off the walls all over the house.

By the time they had finished, they had discovered a Monet beneath a painting of the Great Lakes freighter, the *Arthur M. Anderson.* Next, they exposed hidden behind a photograph of the Harbor Beach Lighthouse a small sketch by John Marin, and finally when they removed the back of a watercolor of the Mackinac Bridge, they uncovered a 6x9 graphite by Salvador Dali. Now it became clear how Mary had become financially independent.

Most of the items that had been sold that fateful day have been returned, but once in awhile a stranger knocks at the door with an object to return and a story to tell. Emma smiles, listens, and waves goodbye to another believer in the ghost of Aunt Mary.

Mike and Em love the peaceful setting of the old house and the privacy it offers them. The sale of one painting brought enough money to live comfortably in the mansion for a very long time. They wondered how many Aunt Mary had sold through the years. It remains a house full of treasures.

Chapter 15

Myth of a Bus Tour to Eternity

People arrived early to board the bus to the Casino located about three hours away. It was a cold, snowy morning, but the bus filled with people happy to leave their everyday mid-winter doldrums. The ride there was uneventful, but the ride back was not. There is a story about that bus, but whether it is true or not cannot be verified.

According to the local tale, the weather quickly deteriorated as the journey continued past small towns and villages. Soon, the road was a blur of white, and as the bus driver strained to see the oncoming traffic, he did not see the deer crossing the road. The bus jumped as it hit the animal causing the vehicle to spin out of control. Landing on its side in a deep culvert, its exits blocked, caused the death of twelve travelers.

Today, people talk about this bus still traveling its same route. They have seen it stop at the required pick-up points. They claim to see its doors open then close although noone is seen getting on or getting off. No one, that is, except vague figures. There are twelve of them; twelve ghostly passengers are seen in the windows as it passes through the small towns and villages on its route to eternity.

Chapter 16

A Haunted Dock?

*f*or many years, as far back as could be remembered, from the early spring up to mid-fall, the Harbor Beach dock would be filled with fishermen. For a time, one of the residents had a bait shop at the foot of the dock where he sold fresh minnows, extra line, sinkers, hooks, and bobbers.

Early spring would find adults lining both sides of the pier pulling jumbo perch from the bay—sometimes even a double header, that is, a line with two hooks with two nice-sized perch on it. Laughter would trickle from one end to the other as friends visited and ate their lunch from paper bags. Sometimes when the fishing slowed, people would get up to stretch their legs with a walk along the wooden boards, stopping to check other buckets for their catch so far that day and asking, "How many you got? Using minnows for bait?"

After school let out for the year, youngsters would find a place to sit on the warm wooden planks that were full of splinters. They were taught by their elders to be quiet on the dock. It was not a playground. As the heat of the summer came on, many wore their swim trucks under their jeans and took a dive into the water, but not from the dock. Never dive from the dock. That was forbidden. Fishing fell off as the waters grew warmer in the summer's sun and the perch headed for the deep cool waters of the bay. They returned at night to feed on the plentiful foods near shore. A few adults with coolers of beer also returned to fish at the very end of the dock.

The Harbor Beach dock

At one time, the dock held little attraction for fishermen, after a few of the of the large manufacturers that once held ownership on the bay managed to completely wipe out any fishing nutrients. This, in turn, killed off the fish populations. In the past, the area north of the dock was filled with black sludge all the way up to the railroad bed on Water Street. It killed huge willow trees, filled the bay with seaweed and carp, and put an end to fishing for many years.

Today the dock holds memories of tanned bodies, buckets filled with yellow belly perch, and long summer days. It is said the perch are back and the dock is once again becoming a haven for assorted fresh water fish and... ghosts?

Once in awhile, a tourist will tell a story to a local about seeing the dock lined with people as they drove their car down the Trescott Street hill, but to their amazement, when they approach the dock on foot, it is empty. Others have told stories of hearing laughter coming from the pier as they near the last piling. Once there they find nothing.

One warm March day this past early spring, two local young ladies set the timer on their camera to take a picture of themselves in the early evening. It seemed the timer was acting unusual, as if it had a mind of its own. Before they could reach the spot where they wanted the picture to be taken, the timer, acting of its own accord went off and had already taken a picture. They tried several times to get good results, but unseen hands were operating the camera's timer. The pictures of what they captured on that day are reproduced here with the permission of the owners. Clearly shown is the spirit of a man standing in front of them? If so, then he wanted his picture taken that day too! Others have reported having difficulty with their camera on the pier; their batteries go dead or bright white lines stretch across their photographs and often a fog carpets the water in the photos when there

Shutter problems?

An apparition or camera problem?

PHOTOS COURTESY OF DANIELLE ROGGENBUCK & MICHELLE TALASKI

is no fog in evidence at the time. One late afternoon, just as a summer thunderstorm approached, a couple posed for a picture. When it was developed, there was a third person with them carrying a fishing pole. It was an older woman wearing a white pull-down hat and a worn blue jacket. She was smiling. Now that's a way to spend eternity!

Rumors of shadow figures darting from the light poles and footsteps following curious visitors circulate through the lakeside villages of Lake Huron. Imagination? Probably. But it does scare you to death when you are down there after dark, walking on that long pier that seems to stretch out into the afterlife.

Chapter 17

Teabury Hill

White painted rocking chairs invite visitors to sit for awhile and listen to the stories of the ghosts that inhabit Teabury Hill.

Ever since the day it was built by a captain that sailed the Great Lakes on ships that carried cargo from Duluth to the southern ports of Lakes Michigan and Erie, it has stunk of evil.

He built the house on Indian burial grounds. The land was owned and homesteaded by his father's father in the early 1800s before the great fires. Before him, it was owned by the Indians who populated this land and built their sacred mounds here. It was a place of sacred legends from its ancient beginnings. The captain was a stubborn man. He built his house here in spite of the neighboring farmer's warnings. He had grown up here on this land and played on the Indian mounds that lay hidden in the forests. He had dug out bones and ancient artifacts with his father who sold them to the tinker man. He remembered the stories of Indian spirits walking the land told to him by his father. They didn't frighten him nor cause him to pause.

Both of his parents had died in the fire of 1881, at a time when the last of the Indians were seen traveling in a long procession of canoes leaving this area for an island along the St. Clair River in Canada. They never returned. They too believed the land was cursed.

He lived with an uncle and aunt until he reached the age when he could make his way of his own free will. Then he left the land to sail the great ships. In time, with money in his pocket, he returned to build his home on the land of his father. He built it of stone to protect it from fires. Unknowingly, he lined the basement with limestone; today it is known to attract spirits. It was a huge house that he only returned to during the winter months, the off season of shipping, safe from the monster winter winds and sea witches that sent ships and their crews to rot on the bottom of the lakes. He built cupboards and closets with winding passages behind them to cause any lingering spirits from the land difficulty in settling in, that is, finding a permanent home in his house. Although he did not believe in the stories told and retold about this place, stories that grew into legends and myths, he was wary of them and always felt unseen eyes upon him.

He built large fireplaces of field stone in the living areas: the parlors, bedrooms, and kitchen to keep away the winter cold and the cold brought from possible phantom visitors. Spiritualism was in its heyday during this time, and he allowed séances to be held in the home in hopes of contacting his father. He hoped his father might help him put the Indian spirits, that he denied seeing roaming the hallways, to rest. They didn't frighten him. Unwelcome guests, he complained.

He brought Mary to Teabury after the house was completed. Mary, a young woman from a northern port fell in love with him at first sight. Barely thirty, the captain was captivated by her sweet charms. They married, he tall and handsome in his captain's uniform and Mary beautiful in her white lace gown with a veil covered with spring flowers. Both were happy, but not forever—no, not forever.

He brought her to his home on a summer voyage and left her there assuring her he would return in November. He gave her permission to decorate their home in any manner she chose and found her a village lady to cook and clean and help with the chores and, so Mary would not spend days and nights alone, he hired a companion to live at the home. She was quiet, a woman who chose to live on the third floor away from the footsteps and shadows that plagued the downstairs rooms. All through the summer as his ship voyaged up and down the lakes, his thoughts were on Mary and their reunion. This winter layover would not be long, not with Mary at his side. He read every one of her letters over and over again thinking of their future together.

November came. The captain on horseback fought his way through the snow drifts that blocked the lane to the house. He worried for there was no sign of life, no wagon tracks or smoke from the many chimneys. The windows were dark—no lamps lit his way as he approached the door.

He found Mary at the foot of the stairway wearing her wedding dress and holding his picture in her hand that clutched at her heart. Her blonde hair spilled over her shoulders and covered the Indian beads that were wrapped tightly around her neck, the same type of Indian beads that were sewn into the lace of her gown. That spring, he buried her next to the yellow tea rose bushes that grew wild along the side of the house. The companion was found in the upstairs bedroom, frozen in a wing-backed chair. Frightened to death? The village cook disappeared into the forests of the land and was never heard of again.

The captain's ship was lost in the storms of 1912 off the coast of Alpena. He saw Mary before he died, her arms full of yellow tea roses as the waves brought his ship and crew to never be seen again.

The Teabury House remains today as a historical site on a bluff overlooking the lake. The spirit of the companion wearing a gray dress with white collar and cuffs is reportedly seen in the dining room and on the second floor stairway. Pots and pans are moved about in the kitchen, and place settings in the dining room are sometimes found scattered on the table. Has the cook also returned? Mary and the captain are often seen in the hallways of the house or sitting in the parlor where the petals of yellow tea roses are evidence of their most recent visit.

The present owners of Teabury have requested their location not be given in this story.

Chapter 18

The Glowing Tombstone

*B*lack wrought-iron fencing wraps around the cemetery behind the abandoned church. The large iron gates are locked tight to keep intruders out—or to keep the occupants in? Passersby are often startled by visions of phantoms moving along the overgrown paths.

The graveyard is one of the oldest in the county with headstones dating back to the early fires that consumed this area time and time again. Should you decide to search for souls locked here by tragedy, go in the early evening before the risings, before 3:00 AM.

It was just 3:00 AM when Sylvia and her friend, Joann, went on a dare one night in mid-summer. It was a hot and humid night when they climbed over the wrought-iron fence just stopping long enough for Sylvia to free her pant leg caught on a twisted piece of metal or something that seemed to pull her back. Ignoring the slight tug, they entered the graveyard near the heavily-rusted, locked back gates that once opened to allow the hearse to drive through to make a deposit. Sylvia's gruff voice, always needling Joann, urged her, "Get off the damn fence and let's go. I want to find that tombstone that is supposed to glow." Slightly overweight, she puffed as she climbed the incline with Joann following behind her. "Do you see anything?" she called as she stopped and leaned against a tall narrow headstone.

"Not really," answered Joann. "It's just too dark."

"Well then, that stone should be easy to see if it glows in the dark," grumbled Sylvia sarcastically as she turned to go farther up the hill. "I always knew that story was a bunch of bunk. I never found anything in the history of this area that gave any evidence of a stone glowing in the dark out here. Just rumors," she wheezed. And Sylvia was never wrong.

Joann followed the flashlight beam to a tall narrow tombstone marker; she stood listening as Sylvia's rantings slowly faded over the hill. She noticed a black horse engraved in the stone, and as she did she felt a blanket of cold air wrap around her. Her eyes adjusted to the flashlight beam as she peered at the faded script:

Stop here not to pray.
These souls have lost their way.
Evil never rests.

Joann shivered and tried to see through the curtain of darkness that enveloped her. What does that mean, *Evil never rests?* Reminds me of Sylvia, she never rests until she is right. She has to always be right.

Meanwhile, Sylvia continued to search for the glowing tombstone. As she started to circle the cemetery, she noticed a beam of light to her right, and, thinking it was Joann, she made her way past grave markers of every size. Her flashlight darted over them as she tried to locate the source of the beam. Suddenly, she felt icy goose bumps cover her arms. Chills spread up her back and neck. She stopped and called, "Joann! Where are you?" Then again she spotted the light beam, now to her left and behind her. "Damn," she muttered to herself, "I walked right by it. If that's Joann, why didn't she call to me? Dumb. She has always been the dumbest woman on the planet." She reached the pinnacle of the cemetery. She shone the beam in a large circle all around her. She was surrounded by tombstones... that seemed to move? No, that's impossible, she thought. "Joann!" she shouted. "Joann!" Then she saw her, walking up the hill toward her, but what was she wearing? "Joann, hurry up! There is nothing here. Let's get out of here!" her voice fading into the darkness as she watched the specter approach her through the overgrown weeds that covered the path. It wasn't Joann. It held its arms out to her—as if welcoming her.

She turned and ran, down the hill, fought again with the fence and ran until she finally found the car with Joann in it and all the doors locked. "Damn-it, Joann, open the door!" she screamed.

The two women never mentioned their foray into the old cemetery to anyone, not even at card club that week where Sylvia always held court. But not this time. This time Sylvia was unusually quiet, her mouth turned down at the corners, her eyes twitching behind her glasses. After the cemetery visit, Joann knew she wasn't really her friend. She soon distanced herself from Sylvia as she remembered, *Evil never rests.*

Is Your House Haunted?

1. Do you hear the sounds of footsteps or perhaps the moving of furniture?
2. Do doors open or close by themselves?
3. Do you smell a favorite perfume or the smell of baking cookies… or anything that reminds you of someone that has passed?
4. Do you seem to lose important items only to have them reappear in an area that you had already searched?
5. Does the TV or radio turn on or off by itself?
6. Is there a window or a door that will not stay closed?
7. Do pets such as dogs or cats seem afraid to enter certain areas of the house?
8. Do you sometimes catch a movement out of the corner of your eye or an unexplained shadow in a room or hallway?
9. Do clocks stop without reason?
10. Have you heard someone whisper your name when no one is home?
11. Do you feel sometimes as if you are being watched?
12. Do photographs taken in the house often appear with unexplainable white mists or orbs appearing in them?
13. Do the batteries die in your camera and regain power after you have left the area?
14. Have you experienced the sensation of someone sitting on your bed or pulling on your covers?
15. Do certain areas of the home feel unusually cold without reason?
16. Have there been any tragic in the house or the grounds upon which it is built?

If you have answered yes to several of these questions, it is quite possible you have a spirit sharing your home.

Contributors

Thank you to the following people that helped in providing me with historical facts, photographs, and permission to retell their experiences with the paranormal. Honoring the request of the many others to remain anonymous is my pleasure.

Catherine Shubitowski
Christmas Spirit
Photograph

Sandi Mager
The Deer Camp Spirit

Brad Blair
The Deer Camp Spirit
Photographs

Mark Bolen
Spirits of the Whitefish Point Lighthouse
Professional Photographer
(mark.bolen@att.net)

The Upper Peninsula Paranormal Society
Spirits of the Whitefish Point Lighthouse
Ghost Hunters
(www.upprs.net)

Julia Chaperone
Sweet Dreams Inn Victoria Bed & Breakfast
Owner

Arthur Schlichting
The Loop-Harrison Mansion
Sanilac Historical Society

Ray & Connie Garrett
The Forester Inn
Owners

Stacy Koss
Point aux Barques Lighthouse

David & Barb Osentoski
Osentoski Real Estate and Auctioneering

Danielle Roggenbuck & Michelle Talaski
A Haunted Dock?
Photographs

About the Author

Janice Langley, author and illustrator, was born in Harbor Beach, Michigan, located on the shores of Lake Huron. She grew up with the sound of the Harbor Beach light's foghorn in the background. She is the mother of three grown children and the wife of Richard J. Langley. They lived in Michigan's Upper Peninsula for forty years, and since Richard's retirement, they have returned to Jan's hometown of Harbor Beach.

If you have experienced paranormal activity and live in the U.P. or in the Thumb area, please contact the author at www.michiganghoststories.net or jan@thecaptainandharry.com.